Breaking Free

Breaking Free

Rescuing Families from the Clutches of Legalism

David R. Miller

BAKER BOOK HOUSE
Grand Rapids, Michigan 49516

Library of Congress Cataloging-in-Publication Data

Miller, David R., 1941–
    Breaking free! : rescuing families from the clutches of legalism /
David R. Miller.
        p.   cm.
    ISBN 0-8010-6288-8
    1. Family—Religious life. 2. Law (Theology)—Controversial
literature. 3. Law and gospel. 4. Christian life—1960– I. Title. II.
Title: Legalism.
    BV4526.2.M47   1992
    248.4—dc20   91-35648

Contents

Preface

Legalism is a "schism" that can afflict, and in fact has afflicted, most religions.

Legalism is the adding of basic presuppositions to a faith to make that faith more exclusive or less available to "outsiders" who do not think, act, or believe as do the "true" believers. Legalism is one of many power maneuvers by faith leaders who seek to consolidate religious authority in the hands of a very few.

Christian legalism in recent years has taken root and grown in response to the very real degeneration of faith and morals, and is most noticeable in Western Europe and North America. Christian legalism found a fertile seedbed in the exclusivity and retreatism of American fundamentalism, but has long since overgrown the hedges of any one form of Christianity. Christian legalism is seen in many groups who enthusiastically add rules and regulations to what traditionally has been standard Christian practice.

The best definition of legalism is that which emanates from the mouth of Jesus, recorded in Matthew's Gospel, chapter 15 verses 8 and 9: "This people draweth nigh unto me with their mouth, and honoreth me with their lips; but their heart is far from me. But in vain do they worship me, *teaching for doctrines the commandments of men*" (italics added).

While most Christians have dealt to some degree with legalism, this book especially will be concerned with the more unhealthy extremes of legalism. It is written primarily to the families who have followed strong authoritarian individuals or groups into legalism, but should also help those legalistic leaders understand themselves and those they affect.

Introduction

Legalism is a snare for Christians, but it is for many a soft, warm, comfortable snare, one that feels safe and is secure as long as things are going well. Legalism, with the need for spiritual security that lies behind it, is an opiate for many Christians, a spiritual narcotic designed to compensate for a largely graceless form of religious belief. Legalism offers Christian families security as long as they practice what a church, Christian institution, or authority figure commands. To parents legalism promises children who will grow up straight and strong with firm convictions to guide them through life.

And legalism, in the short term and under special circumstances, can deliver on these promises. It would be a mistake to believe that Christian legalism has no merit. It has merit and can deliver—but at a very heavy price.

Sin is tempting because it's often fun, at least in the short term. Similarly, legalism, although not so much fun, is comfortable, reassuring, and safe. Legalism works to keep things under control and to give an appearance of goodness—well-behaved children for proud parents to show off or a well-ordered life with no hint of the turmoil shaking the foundation.

"No rebels here! Not my kids! Not in my three-times-a-week-to-church family with our well-known pastor and our strong 'fellowship.'"

"No radical, weirdo, homosexual, flag-burning, long-haired, drug-crazed, Krishna-chanting degenerates coming out of *our* families and churches and schools."

Such parents are usually right about this.

But the absence of obvious "degenerates" doesn't necessarily mean everything is great. Facing legalistic Christian families are other less obvious problems, but problems with equal or greater potential for damage than the excesses of liberal religion or no religion at all.

Legalistic Christians have their own "gurus," authority figures in church or Christian college happy to prescribe rules for living. They will say why beards on men are not "Christian," why slacks on women are not "Christian," why divorced people are not allowed to sing in the choir or serve as ushers.

Certain camps of conservative and legalistic Christianity go so far as to institute "morality police" scattered throughout the Christian community who informally are encouraged to keep an eye on alumni, church members, and other preachers and speakers, then to report back to "headquarters."

Authority figures have answers for everything. Families have good feelings about themselves, but no freedom to question. And parents will be asked difficult questions one day.

"Why could we not do this or that?"

"Who said it was good or bad?"

"Were those rules Bible based or just the preferences of an authority figure somewhere?"

"Mom and Dad, who was in charge of this family when we were growing up?"

Tough questions, but reality based.

My family and I know what legalism feels like, what it does to family members. We know the "warm fuzzies" of conforming to a legalistic setting, and we know the depth of pain when unusual things confront a family, things outside the ability of those warm fuzzies to fix.

I do not presume to speak for all people who have experienced a legalistic form of Christianity. I recognize that legalism sometimes works for families in the system, families who for any number of reasons are not called upon to deal with the more difficult issues of Christian living. They are happy in legalism. Their children do not ask difficult questions and perhaps will not.

What I write is a reflection of my family's experiences and our growing concern for those trying to break free and recover from the oppression that accompanies legalism.

I do not try to persuade Christians to change their lifestyles or leave a church, mission board, or Christian college or university. My purpose is that of a counselor, which is my profession, and what I feel God has called me to do.

I am now free of any need for "getting even" with the legalists of my past, the authority figures who did their best to control and direct every aspect of the Miller family's life. That's over.

My purpose is to comfort, show compassion, stimulate careful thought, and encourage healing. I will suggest options that may have been off-limits to Christian families in the past.

This is not a "how-to-live" book. To try to write one would be not only foolish but arrogant as well.

I will, however, suggest that no authority figure, pastor, college president, television evangelist, nor anyone else has the right to tell other Christians how they should manage their families. I certainly acknowledge the need for preaching and teaching the Word of God, but as distinct from the word of men. The gray areas of Christian living are best left to the individual families themselves, and God has promised his Holy Spirit to help in their "discerning" matters.

I will tell of my experiences and those of my family. They include being in five Bible-preaching fundamental/ evangelical churches and two Christian universities of the same doctrinal position but at different levels of legalism. I will also offer anecdotes and real-life lessons experienced by friends and counseling clients who have shared their experiences with me.

Legalism is found in other forms of religions around the world. Who could be more legalistic than Shi'ite Moslems who will cut off a hand for stealing and a head for adultery? The veiled faces on women who are forbidden to drive automobiles parallel Christian legalism that teaches women should be "in their place" and not competitive with men. No group is more in favor of capital punishment than legalistic Christians, except maybe those Shi'ite Moslem legalists.

The required prayer by Hindu believers is matched by the almost daily attendance at services by legalistic Christians, and the caste system of India is paralleled by the skirt measuring, facial hair forbidding, divorcee excluding of many legalistic Christian groups. Dress codes at some Christian colleges are matched by the imposition of a dress code in the Punjab section of India, where recently the majority religious element legislated a death penalty for men who trim their beards and for women who wear western-style clothing. Mormons are legalistic in their requirement for building genealogies and for a "family night" once a week. Jehovah's Witnesses express legalism with their "voluntary but required" door knocking and pamphlet passing, activities one speaker called "religious mugging."

No, legalism is not unique to Christianity.

All families and all religions are vulnerable to the excesses of legalism, and anyone identifying with such a religion is a potential recruit for the "morality police" always found in legalistic groups.

Yes, we know that legalism emphasizes externals more than internals, while it proclaims just the opposite. Legalists of all stripes are comfortable with the idea that to observe a person's behavior is to know that person's character, while they ignore the motives behind the conformity.

Legalism preaches, whether implicitly or explicitly, the importance of each one watching another—to keep each other close to the Lord of course, but watching, nevertheless. Frequently it encourages reporting back to an authority figure so the "body of believers" can be kept pure.

Legalism is a perversion of true Christianity. In examining it Christians must ask themselves if they have assigned their God-given freedom to run their lives and manage their families according to their understanding of God's leading over to an authority figure. Being freed from Christian legalism means going back to the freedom God has promised in true Christianity. Being free means that each Christian today can expose the secret pharisee hiding in all, just as Jesus helped his people to do in the days he walked the earth.

Being free from legalism does not mean our family has changed our religious beliefs, but rather that we no longer have to look outside our own family and our own Bible for direction. Our lives are still consistently Christian, still conservative and evangelical, but now for different reasons.

What Linda and I do now, and what our grown children do, or do not do, derives from personal conviction and sound Bible teaching rather than the preferences of a Christian leader presuming to know our family better than we know ourselves. Our convictions about hair length, clothing, music, movies, reading material, and a hundred other gray areas give our lives structure and direction. We are free to answer God's call on our lives without checking with an authority figure first.

Our church affiliation and denominational identity has not changed in thirty years, but we are free of legalism. Our Lord has not changed, nor has the Bible, but we are free of legalism.

It is *we* who have changed, and for the better!

Being free from the security trap of legalism is the most refreshing and invigorating experience we could have imagined. It is our testimony that such freedom can only be found in Jesus. We have freedom from artificial restraints and penalties for infractions, but also we have obtained freedom to love and care about people regardless of where they go to church or how they wear their hair.

It will not be necessary for me to identify any church, Christian college, or other Christian organization. There is no shortage of legalistic Christian colleges and universities, as well as churches and para-church organizations. Some are striving mightily to break free of the legalistic traditions of many years, and many are succeeding. Others are moving in the other direction, retreating even further behind the barricades to await the end times.

Therefore, this book is not about one school or one authority figure. It is about family, how to understand what can happen in legalism, and how to protect families from this aberration of true Christianity.

1

The Irrationality of Legalism

I am a recovering legalist. My wife, Linda, and I would be charter members of "Legalists Anonymous" if there were such an organization

Being in recovery means that I accept my own struggles as well as the struggles of other Christians as necessary steps in the process of breaking free. It would be no more appropriate for me to belittle the battles faced by a person at a different stage of breaking away from legalism than for a recovering alcoholic to poke fun at a person who slips off the wagon once in a while.

Legalism has much in common with alcoholism and any other kind of addiction. Consider the commercials for alcohol on television.

"Drink our beer and you will be popular, sound intelligent, and the opposite sex will find you irresistible. Drink our beer and your life will be a ball, full of fun and great times. Don't worry. Be happy!"

The "commercials" for legalism delivered on Christian radio and television, through countless sectarian newspapers, and in legalistically oriented churches have a similar but more spiritual message.

"Join our church and you will be happy. Life will be a spiritual 'blast'! But you can only get this kind of joy here, nowhere else. Send your kids to our Christian college or university and they will turn out right. On our campus we make sure they stay where you want them."

"Be like us. That's all; just be like us. Don't ever deviate from the shining path that only we can see. Don't question or complain, because God has shown us that this is *the* way Christian people are to live. Don't worry. Be happy!"

Well, it's time for Christians to worry some about the impact of legalism.

I base this premise on my twenty years in Christian legalism and fifteen years' experience as a Christian counselor to families. There will be pain in my words, but I am reminded that growth only comes from a sense of discomfort. I offer them in sincere love and in the confident hope that God can heal any wound.

I will try to explain what legalism does to individuals, families, and Christian leaders. My experience is that once legalism gains control of a ministry, two results are most likely. One, the children in the families become overwhelmed with the restrictions and requirements of a legalistic lifestyle. The need to conform is so strong in legalistic systems that children become well-behaved, obedient in the extreme, but with their individuality, creativity, and curiosity smothered by the demands of the system.

The second result is at least equally dangerous. Leaders in legalistic systems eventually begin to see themselves as more than mere leaders. They go through an ego transformation that tells them they must be more than the others, better, more spiritual, with fewer failings and temptations. Legalism teaches that externals reveal internals, and its leaders first evolve into Christian detectives, looking for that raised hemline or hair over the collar that will reveal what this person or that is "really" like on the inside. In the end such legalistic Christian leaders become monsters through the abuses of power that always follow this philosophy.

For example, we can sense the arrogance of some television evangelists as they wrap themselves in American flags and wave their Bibles. The power drive of these preachers grows as they tell their audiences to stand up or sit down, repeat after them, and answer yes or no on their commands. In the extreme they become enamored with their power to draw money to their ministries, and the lure of "living like kings" leads to gold-plated bathroom fixtures in multi-million dollar homes scattered across the country. Obviously, power can corrupt Christian leaders as any other leaders.

Hence, ordinary Christians become mice who allow their leaders to become beneficent monsters, Christian dictators, Bible-based ayatollahs who can't wait to add their own "interpretations" to traditional Christian teachings so they can be separate and establish that City on the Hill.

"Don't worry. Be happy!"

The Importance of Ideas

God tells us in the first book of the Bible that "the wickedness of man was great in the earth, and that every imagination of the thoughts of his heart was only evil continually" (Gen. 6:5).

We live and die by the thoughts of our hearts. Thought as well as soul distinguishes humans from the lower creatures. Thoughts control us, define us, energize and direct our actions, and bring us either closer to God or lead us to flee from him.

Legalistic Christians think differently from other Christians. They are no less intelligent or less educated necessarily. They think differently from nonlegalistic Christians because they have perverted their ideas by deviating from the directions God has commanded or by adding human preferences to what God has commanded.

This is the error of legalism. Legalism adds individual or corporate preferences to God's Word and places these man-made additions on an equal standing with God's Word.

Legalism has been present in some form or other throughout the history of the church. For example, the Roman Catholic church once practiced the selling of indulgences, just as now some elements of conservative Protestantism "sell" prayer cloths, healing water, and promises to pray. This reveals the power drive in such Protestant leaders as effectively as the offering of indulgences revealed the power of the church in the Middle Ages. As one branch of Christianity demanded works to enter heaven, so another branch demands a person's expression of spiritual "gifts," behavioral conformity to an extra-biblical standard of living, and exclusive involvement in one church as evidence of salvation.

Why do Christians allow their minds to be controlled by legalistic authority figures? Why do some of them accept unquestionably the right of another human being to tell them that his thoughts on Christian living are more powerful than their own? It usually does not happen suddenly, but subtly and over a period of time legalistic Christians are influenced to assimilate some irrational ideas into their own thinking.

Irrational Idea 1:
A Christian should be dependent
upon an authority figure

Christians living in legalism have allowed themselves to be persuaded to trust a human authority figure who can logically and persuasively convince others of his right to lead. Every legalist is a conformist with a deep need to test the wind to see which way the spiritual authority breezes blow and then to move with the breeze rather than against it. All legalistic Christians, those who value externals more than internals, expect others to tell them what they should do and how they should think.

Walking out of a particularly contentious chapel service a few years ago, I overheard a student say to another student, "I didn't know that's what *we* believe. Did you?" Apparently he was willing to become submerged in this kind of cognitive surrender.

Many of us Christians have heard surprising statements coming from a church pulpit, often by a visiting evangelist or other guest speaker. In my former church it was common to have a guest preacher or speaker occasionally on Sunday evening. One Sunday our pastor introduced "Dr." Williams to the congregation and commented that he was an old and dear friend from Bible college days. Dr. Williams had acquired his doctorate in the manner typical of legalistic Christianity, as an honorary degree from a Bible school somewhere.

Dr. Williams began with the compulsory bad joke and quickly moved to his main topic for the evening. He announced to his captive church audience that he had personal and irrefutable evidence that the makers of a well-known cola were "bankrolling" most of the pornography industry in this country. However, he did not reveal any source of his astounding data to the congregation that evening, and years have passed with none of his charges being supported. But he went on ad nauseam as to why "real" Christians would not buy that brand of soft drink.

The reader may well question if anyone in his or her right mind would believe such drivel, and wonder what the problem is. Remember that this was a legalistic church where people had been taught that no one challenges "God's man." Members simply do not question authority figures in legalistic churches or organizations without running the risk of someone questioning their spirituality.

I know from personal conversations with the pastor that he also thought the comments on the cola were ridiculous and was actually embarrassed by them, but he never expressed those thoughts to the congregation. Why? Because to have challenged one of God's servants, even when apparently justified, *might* have taught others that it would be okay to challenge the pastor himself on other issues. This pastor, an admitted and proud legalist, could not bring the truth about these crazy comments to light because of the risk that "his" people might turn their critical thinking in his direction one day.

Now, how does this kind of thinking affect the family? I have found myself on many occasions counseling Christian parents, usually the father, about discipline. The case involving Al Dwyer had to do with one Christian father and his confrontation with legalistic teachings.

Al's concern was with his thirteen-year-old son Kevin, but it related heavily to what was going on at his church. It was really Al's confusion over the adult Sunday school class he and his wife had been attending that motivated this Christian dad to want to talk with someone.

The Dwyers were members of a large, independent, fundamental/evangelical church in the city. This church had an excellent reputation for solid Bible teaching and preaching and was not known for being legalistic. But in spite of the pastor not being legalistic, it was legalistic teaching in the adult class that was creating problems for Al.

For about four years Bob Freeman had been the teacher of the "Solid Rock" adult Sunday school class. Bob had joined the church staff after graduating from a seminary known to be prone to legalism, but had apparently been able to avoid conflict so far with the other pastors on staff.

Among much good, acceptable doctrinal teaching being done by Bob Freeman, he had apparently begun to go off on what old timers used to call "rabbit trails" in his lessons. Bob was teaching that the only acceptable way to discipline children was with a rod of some kind, that it was "unbiblical" to refuse to spank or to spank with a hand instead of a rod or stick. Bob had even gone so far as to suggest the number of strokes necessary for children at different ages, the greater number being saved for older children like thirteen-year-old Kevin, Al's son.

Kevin was not a stranger to trouble, but Al and his wife felt that Kevin was too old for physical punishment. Even though they had their own feelings on what was best for Kevin, Al had agreed to go along with Bob's teaching and continue spanking his son when he misbehaved.

The result was that Kevin had run away.

He was found at a friend's house and brought home, but he said that if he was spanked again he would kill himself. The embarrassment was too much, Kevin said, and he would rather die than be humiliated like that again.

What was Al supposed to do?

Should he continue to follow the instruction of a trained Bible teacher? Or should he listen to his own heart on the matter?

Of course, Kevin was not the real problem in this true story; it was Al's uncertainty of how to deal with legalistic teachings that came into conflict with his own Spirit-led conscience as a Christian father.

We examined the Bible passages Bob had said justified his conclusions and found there were problems when context was taken into account. We found that the Bible has many things to say about personal and family discipline, but the overriding emphasis is that parents are to be responsible for family discipline to be administered in wisdom and love.

Parents. Period.

What helped Al was that he found the freedom to do what he felt right, balanced with clear biblical teachings. But this was only a partial answer for Al. He wanted to know what was wrong with him that he should have been so easily persuaded in the first place. How could he have been talked into giving his parental authority to this person who knew almost nothing about Kevin or his family?

Al and I eventually realized that it had been a combination of things working together that had brought his family to this point. Al and his wife had become Christians as young adults and had immediately joined a solid, Bible-believing church, one that would only later become known for its legalistic stand on issues. The Dwyers had been taught to accept authority as new Christians, and they had never known anything else.

The Dwyers changed Sunday school classes and spoke with the pastor about their reasons for doing so. Apparently the pastor talked with Bob Freeman about "rabbit trails," and the excesses of his lessons diminished. Bob was a good teacher and a fine Christian who seemed to need only a little encouragement to give up many of his personal preferences and get back to teaching the Bible alone.

But what happened to the Dwyers can happen to anyone taught to trust human leadership more than themselves when it comes to family concerns. Al was not doing "what was right in his own eyes," because instead he was asking Bible teachers and counselors for guidance, discussing his decisions with Christians he trusted. Like so many Christians trapped in a legalistic setting, Al became dependent on an authority figure. His victory came through careful, prayerful consideration of the freedom of each Christian to follow the leadership of the Holy Spirit in the "gray" areas of family life. He no longer simply asked others to tell him what he should do.

Irrational Idea 2:
It is easier and more Christian
to avoid conflicts with the world
than to face them

There are two basic philosophies of Christian education. One is that children and young people should be protected from the outside world while they are "in training" so they will be well prepared, spiritually equipped, and relatively uncontaminated when they leave the fold and enter the real world. This is sometimes called the "hothouse" philosophy, the premise being that growing things will turn out stronger, more attractive, and more like one another than those raised in a less controlled environment.

The second may be called the "bend-with-the-wind" philosophy. This is education within a "low hedge," providing minimal protection and controlled exposure to the world. The thinking behind this point of view is that young people become stronger and more resistant to contamination if they have, with guidance, faced some of the "winds and pressures" common to their environment. This second approach also emphasizes protection but with gradual and increasing exposure to the problems and pressures of everyday Christian living.

Legalistic Christian parents, churches, and institutions are more likely to be of the "hothouse" orientation. This perspective has advantages, not the least of which is that parents feel less worried about what their children are doing, because generally they *know* what their children are doing or not doing.

But there are disadvantages as well. Some have taken this hothouse idea to the point of protecting their young even from other Christians only slightly different from themselves. Small Christian schools connected to single churches are the usual result of this thinking. It has been my experience and is shown in some research that parents who home school tend to be of the most extreme form of legalistic orientation. I know of home schoolers who even attend church in their own living rooms.

On the face of it home schooling may appear laudable. Isn't it great to do things as a family? Isn't it refreshing to see Mom doing the teaching and Dad doing the preaching? What a wonderful family they must be!

But is it really so great?

Granted, some parents can provide excellent home schooling, but as with too sheltered or narrowly defined Christian day schools the danger exists that the lack of experience with those unlike themselves will lead to culture shock and overwhelm those students when they go out into the real world.

I have had dozens of students from home schools sit in my office in anger and tears realizing how poorly educated they were at home, totally unprepared for the rigors of college level work, angry at parents who loved them but did not allow them to be properly prepared for life.

There are as many varieties of Christian colleges and universities as one could possibly wish for, ranging from very liberal in theology and moral standards for students and faculty to those that are little more than fortresses of the faith, where the students secured inside have almost no personal freedom to make choices.

There is no question that the more legalistic, barricade-mentality schools experience fewer moral casualties with their students, at least while they *are* students. If protection is the prime concern for parents, legalism has the schools to guarantee protection.

But what happens after graduation? The defend-the-faith mentality, honorable in its own right, somehow produces Christians more willing to retreat when confronted than to take the offensive. Yet, Christianity today has greater need of warriors than defenders, soldiers trained for battle rather than mice trained to run and hide to protect their "purity" at the expense of a lost world.

But it is not only in education that legalism's protective mentality prevails. Adult mice need leaders to tell them what to do, giving rise to a whole group of "Protestant Popes" assuming for themselves the power to tell people how to dress, act, with whom they may associate, which books they may read and which are off limits. Such adult mice who are out in the world tend to be smugly self-righteous in their perceived superior morality over their neighbors and co-workers. At the end of the day they retreat to their safe homes and church activities.

Irrational Idea 3:
There is a correct and precise answer to every question

Legalists fear ambiguity.

Safety and security are prime movers for legalistic Christians, not challenge and opportunity.

There is no security in the gray areas of life, no safety in the unknown. Black and white are good, clear, understandable, and identifiable: safe.

Legalists seek answers, not challenges. However, legalists do not like searching for answers, spiritual or otherwise. Rather, they feel comfortable in being *told* what is true and correct by people they believe they can trust.

If an answer appears unlikely, the fault lies in the person doing the searching. There *must* be an answer; we know that God is not a God of confusion, don't we? So, if a person is confused about something, the fault must lie with that person, not the nature of the problem. To a legalist an ambiguity is a sign of failure, a pain stimulus in need of anesthesia.

Legalism is the morphine that numbs the pain of uncertainty.

Nonlegalistic Christians are better able to accept the fact that the Bible does not speak to every specific concern of modern life. Legalists will give lip-service agreement to this idea, but their lives give them away. They worry, they fail to trust the Holy Spirit to lead them through the grayness of the unknown. There must be an answer for every problem. After all, God is perfect and the Bible is inerrant, so where is the answer? There must be an answer.

Legalism offers answers to its adherents. If a clear answer is not to be found in the Bible, leadership will simply proclaim an answer to the people, and the people will accept it. I know; I have been there. And it really feels good knowing there are answers for everything.

But a time comes when the man-made answer fails and we realize that God all along expected us to trust and obey him and his Holy Spirit in spite of the gray surrounding us at the time.

Nonlegalistic Christians are unafraid of scholarly theology or debate and argument. They are ready to dig for answers not apparent on the surface. Whereas legalistic leaders tell people the verses *they* believe will meet the needs, nonlegalistic Christians are more likely to say, "Sit down. Tell me what's on your mind. We'll pray about it and search the Scripture, and then *you* can decide what you should do."

Legalism is the morphine of fearful Christianity.

Irrational Idea 4:
A Christian should be completely competent, adequate, and an achiever to be worthwhile

Neither legalistic nor nonlegalistic Christians have the monopoly on making mistakes. They deal with their mistakes differently.

Is a mistake at work a chastening from God, or just a mistake at work?

Was that fender bender I had at the mall last week a message from God, or my poor driving?

How these everyday questions are answered can usually be predicted if a person's stand on legalism is known. Given a legalist's tendency to evaluate spirituality by examining appearance, behavior, and social interaction it is no great stretch to find negative reactions when mishaps occur. What legalistic Christians do to others, they do to themselves. When reminded that we are only to judge others as we would be judged, legalists agree, because they *do* judge themselves in the same harsh manner as others.

In counseling legalistic Christians in some kind of trouble, the very first words I usually hear are, "What did I do to deserve this?"

George Canelli was an afflicted man, even though most of his suffering was self-inflicted. George and his wife, Elaine, had joined our church and began to attend the adult Sunday school class in which Linda and I were active. They seemed friendly and outgoing, a normal couple as far as was noticeable.

Within a few months of our first meeting, George stayed after church one morning and asked if he could talk with me privately. His facial expression told me there was something very serious on his mind.

We found am empty office in which to talk, and George quickly told me that he was experiencing some very real self-doubt about his relationship with God and his feelings about himself. We had talked casually about family and background, and George knew about our experiences in legalism. Legalism was on George's mind that morning.

With much hesitation and embarrassment, George told me that his son had just been expelled for the semester from our Christian high school. Brian was nailed for smoking in the boy's bathroom, something done by many other fourteen-year-olds, but not in Christian schools.

This event was obviously more significant for George than for most parents I have known to go through the same experience. Most Christian parents are angry at their teenager and disappointed with his or her behavior, but George seemed more depressed than angry.

On George's mind was the question of what *he* had done wrong. In spite of Brian's sincere repentance and promises to stay out of trouble in the future, his dad was depressed. George was consumed with guilt and a sense of personal failure, because he felt that *he* must have failed as a father for this to happen.

Like me, George was a recovering legalist, but he was not as far along the road to recovery. His family was younger than mine, and Brian was their oldest child. As often happens in families, the first child to enter adolescence is a major cause for concern.

I learned that George had been taught by the pastor of his home church in another state that when a child or teen gets in "serious" trouble, look to the parents and the home for the cause. We talked at length that morning and in several sessions to follow. I wanted to help George think through the question, Why shouldn't Brian get into trouble? Did George and Elaine really think that they were such perfect parents and had such complete control over this young teenager that *they* should be at fault if Brian did wrong?

We looked at many Bible passages, but the one that seemed to help George was Psalm 127. There David talks about children being an inheritance of the Lord who need to be prepared for eventual "nest leaving." George came to see that his attempt to take responsibility on himself for what Brian had done was not only wrong scripturally, but was going to delay Brian's growing up. We agreed that no one raised in a legalistic environment will ever be totally free of the tendency to self-judge, but we can all improve.

What was most encouraging about George and Elaine was their determination to raise their children in a less critical, less judgmental, more accepting home than either of them had experienced. We had talked about mice and monsters earlier, and as our conversation neared conclusion, George told me, with jaw set and eyes determined, that their children would be neither mice nor monsters, but would feel unconditional love in unlimited amounts.

George was able to climb out of the dark valley of Christian legalism and accept his own imperfections. George and Elaine became "good enough" parents as well as recovering legalists.

Irrational Idea 5:
A Christian should be terribly concerned
and fearful about something
that is or may become a problem

Legalists are worriers.

They don't like worrying any more than anyone else and they probably will resist admitting to worrying, but legalistic Christians cannot help worrying.

I mentioned earlier that the security offered by legalism numbs the pain of life's uncertainties, but those unknown and uncontrollable aspects of life are out there anyway. Legalistic Christians make the same claims to trusting God as do nonlegalistic Christians, but for the legalists it is a sham profession.

Legalists are very likely to be traditional and conservative in both religion and politics. The decision to be conservative and traditional was not consciously arrived at, but was adopted unaware as a way of staying safe in the known of the past. Thus, old-time religion is always better than anything done today. The gold standard would save our country from economic ruin, and McGuffey's Readers are still the best teaching tools.

In religious practice this mind-set falls naturally into an apocalyptic view of the end times and is evidenced in the attitude of most legalistic Christians that the world is unredeemable and effort in that direction is wasted.

Man the barricades! Purify our little group of saints, and let the world get its just reward.

This dread of the future fills the home with uncertainty and tells children that they can expect to lose in life. The world, after all, is no friend of grace, and anyone who succeeds out in the world must have compromised somewhere along the way.

Families in legalistic churches and organizations talk like the losers they perceive themselves to be. Many leaders of legalistic schools, churches, and other organizations speak and write as if they were convinced that all efforts to win the world for Jesus are doomed to failure from the beginning, that the world has become so corrupt that even the gospel is falling on deafened ears. Half-hearted invitations to salvation and other spiritual decisions are offered with the enthusiasm of a funeral message.

Legalistic Christians will admit to being isolationists, and they will justify this perspective by arguing that someone has to keep the gospel pure and undefiled. If this preservation can only be done by those who stay away from the corrupting influence of the world, then that will be done. Legalistic Christians will be the first to condemn the cloistering of monks and nuns but will defend their own version of cloistering as necessary.

Legalists are the crustaceans of modern Christianity, wearing their armor on the outside as some crustacean species wear their skeletons on the outside for protection. Each Christian worries only in response to unbelief, but for many Christians the admission of such unbelief is unacceptable. Thus we find legalistic Christians, and even some who are not so legalistic, making bold commitments in public, showing off their armor as it were, but secretly fearful that someone will probe their soft underbellies of spiritual question marks.

Of Course, There's Hope!

Is there hope for legalistic Christians? Absolutely!

George and Elaine came out of legalism. So did Linda and I. The ranks of "Legalists Anonymous" continue to grow, but so do the ranks of legalists. In times of stress and uncertainty, people seek a sanctuary.

The challenge is formidable. Those who care for Christians in pain must rely on prayer as their most powerful medicine. The prayers of others brought our family back to our spiritual senses—prayer and unconditional love.

We must recognize that legalism is as much a snare for Christians as liberalism, and breaking free can be difficult. But the fresh air of knowing a God who accepts us and loves us unconditionally is so pleasant and exhilarating that any risks are small in comparison. No one freed from legalism would ever go back. But those who are free must continue to care for those left behind who still deal with a frightening God who loves them only when they behave themselves. They need compassion.

2

Liberty Lost
Legalism and the Family

Christian legalism can be likened to a virus, a sickness of the body, that can invade any Christian family with devastating results. Legalism is the adding of personal preference to biblical principles and teaching them as equal in authority to the Bible. Legalism was repeatedly condemned by Jesus. Yet legalism enters the body of Christ, the church, infecting and rendering dysfunctional all it touches.

But legalism differs from physical, viral illness in that it is usually contracted voluntarily—a disease of choice for most, a free-will sickness. Those who choose legalism do so because it meets their most basic spiritual or psychological needs in some important way. Such needs may be for security and safety, for acceptance in an exclusive group, or for feeling superior to others. A scholar of the civil rights movement in this country has concluded that many whites who were opposed to equal rights in reality were not opposed to the people but to the loss of their "special" status as "superior" whites. There is no mystery as to why many legalistic Chris-

33

tians are concentrated in all-white churches, all-white neigh-borhoods, and all-white, usually private, schools. Legalism is closely akin to bigotry, be it racial or religious bigotry. Cer-tainly, members of minority groups are also vulnerable to legalism, yet it remains a characteristic of legalism around the world that it is concentrated in the most powerful group.

Children

Many persons are not legalists voluntarily: those born into a family whose parents espouse a legalistic form of Chris-tianity. Children cannot choose their parents, of course, and though legalistic people are often very good parents as the world would judge goodness, there is a corruption in the heart of the legalistic family that will eventually break through the surface and adversely affect the children.

Legalistic parents are extremely unlikely to drink or use drugs, have extramarital affairs, allow pornography into the home, or separate or divorce. The damage comes not from what is done *to* the children but rather through the more subtle messages they learn about themselves and others. They may learn that they are superior to other children, even other Christian children. They may be taught that their church and their form of worship is the only one that pleases God. They may learn that anyone who uses a version of the Bible other than the one approved by their authority figures is somehow less spiritual, less Christian.

Legalism usurps the decision-making liberties of Christians and hands them over to authority figures eager to receive them. Christians may choose to become legalists, but once that choice is made, any remnants of individual freedom to choose are quickly lost. Legalism unchecked will destroy the testimony of a Christian family by making things (appear-ances, associations, choice of school or neighborhood) more important to them than other people.

Legalism turns rational, normal, confident Christians into weaklings who are unable to make choices without official approval. They are willing to believe the most outlandish statements spoken by an authority figure in a church or parachurch organization. Legalism inevitably turns children into church mice and Christian leaders into authoritarian monsters.

A Perversion

Christian legalism is a perversion of Christian love and liberty and is leading great numbers of believers into radical, reclusive, isolated lifestyles. Even violence is a greater danger in legalistic families than in others due to the importance of "testimony."

Legalists believe it necessary to keep family problems—even normal, developmental concerns—away from public knowledge lest "outsiders" think the Christian God is unable to heal a hurting family. Therefore, perhaps it is best to use physical force to get family compliance. Perhaps it is sometimes necessary to beat "a fear of the Lord" into rebellious children or teens, or maybe even a wife. The family exists, legalists believe, to serve the church and not the reverse. Violence is taught in many legalistic families as a necessary and useful evil that may be required by special circumstances.

Legalism is not of God, though legalists believe they are God's special people. Legalism corrupts the necessary love within a family and teaches that authority figures outside the family know best. Legalism teaches that the authoritative position on any subject is universally correct, and to challenge the scriptural basis for decisions made by authority figures is disloyal and lacking in true faith in God.

To challenge authority in a legalistic church or organization is risky business. Thousands of legalistic churches are quick to respond to any challenge to their exclusive brand of Christian living.

The article that prompted this book provoked a firestorm of controversy (so it seemed to me). I was soundly thrashed by several well-known (to legalists) pastors and other leaders.

This was not pleasant, of course. But what made it worthwhile was the other flood of comments I received from people who were also recovering from legalism or were prompted to begin the process.

Challenging a legalistic system is never easy, because it is a system and not just one church or one pastor or leader but a whole network of legalists determined to protect their spiritual purity from all assaults.

But to the extent that legalism is entrenched in my church or yours, or maybe just beginning to take root with the arrival of a new pastor, it is the responsibility of each Christian to do everything reasonable to insure that our children and new converts coming into the church will not be corrupted by the attractiveness of legalism.

The Nature of Legalism

As defined in the previous chapter, legalists are people who add personal preference to accepted doctrinal teaching, accept these additions as having equal weight with doctrinal teaching, and apply these additions in the judging of others. Jesus was concerned enough about this tendency to remind us to "judge not according to the appearance" (John 7:24). Paul, too, was sufficiently interested in warning about legalism when he confronted the Roman church with these words: "Therefore, thou art inexcusable, O man, whosoever thou art that judgest; for wherein thou judgest another, thou condemnest thyself; for thou that judgest doest the same things" (Rom. 2:1).

Legalists are authoritarian in nature. For example, Christian legalists may take the position that because their particular interpretation of the Bible mandates male believers to wear short hair and women to wear theirs long, the next logical step is that the church or institutional authority figure proclaim exactly how long is "long" and how short is "short." The rationale, which is specious at best, is that women and men should not be "confused" in their appearance. I don't know that too many people have struggled to be able to tell males from females because of confusing hairstyles. But I suspect that this rationale is just another way of imposing the will of leaders on "subordinates" in the church.

This tendency applies to many of the "gray" areas of life: what clothing is modest and what is immodest; what movies are acceptable on television; which music is okay or not okay; that it is acceptable to play cards with an "Old Maid" deck but not with standard playing cards (something about the occult, you know).

Finally, this authoritarian disposition to tell others what to do is almost totally a male prerogative. As an example, I offer the following from our family's experience with legalism.

While on the faculty of a large Christian university, I learned from Linda and our daughters that female students, faculty members, even staff had to wear pantyhose all the time. Always. No, not during gym class or under pajamas, but everywhere else and all the time.

This requirement extended all the way down to junior high school girls, which involved one of our daughters. The school was sponsoring an outdoor activity appropriately called an outing, and the girls would be allowed to wear culottes (split skirts) instead of the standard skirts or dresses required for school. Boys could wear blue jeans.

As was the style in those days, all the girls wore knee stockings and were reminded by their teachers that they shouldn't forget to wear pantyhose underneath the culottes.

Pantyhose under knee stockings with culottes? Sounded strange to me. But never underestimate the ability of legalism to make ridiculous rules and take them seriously.

Why did the girls have to wear pantyhose under their culottes? Well, nobody seemed to know for sure, except that the school leadership had decided that this was "modest and appropriate." Male leadership, of course, who did not wear pantyhose.

Now this may seem a small thing, but consider the loss of parental authority that is created when a father or mother in a legalistic setting cannot even begin to explain such rules, and why Mom and Dad are reluctant to ask about it themselves.

Never having been a particularly cautious person, I asked anyway and was told 1) we have always done it that way here; 2) get with the program and stop asking stupid questions.

I was reminded again that legalistic Christians assume the right to tell others how to interpret God's will, even beyond the wearing of pantyhose. Legalists are good authoritarians, being able both to accept and administer dictates. Legalists of any religious orientation do not like questions, because questions are *always* taken as challenges to their authority. If questioning persists, accusations of disloyalty will eventually surface, and even challenges to the questioner's spiritual condition. Don't forget, a good Christian follows "God-given" authority.

Family Impact

Just which freedoms are lost when a family becomes legalistic? I offer the following case from my counseling file as illustration.

Bruce Brown was a friend and colleague at a Christian university where I taught psychology. The Brown family were well known for their fine Christian testimony and the clean-cut appearance and behavior of all four boys. They appeared to be an ideal Christian family from any perspective.

Bruce taught music at the university, and it seemed natural that the boys would develop musical talent, which they did. "The Brown Boys" were a favorite gospel quartet and often performed in local churches and teen camps. They ranged in age from fourteen to twenty at the time, and it was Larry, the oldest, who becomes the focus of this story.

Larry told me that he had been depressed for the first time in his life and didn't feel comfortable telling his mom or dad about it. Such reluctance to share problems is very common in legalistic Christian families, because they have been taught that problems are sin based. This explained why Larry was talking to me instead of his dad.

As Larry related his story, his feelings of depression had begun soon after he started dating Angela, a freshman at this same Christian university. Angela was well known, universally liked, and had the benefit of a spotless reputation, something even more important at a legalistic than at a normal institution.

It seemed the only people unhappy with Larry and Angela were Larry's parents. But Larry felt that being twenty years of age and a senior in college, he was at a point where he could be trusted to know whom to date. Larry was concerned that I know that the relationship was moral and appropriate in every way, and I certainly had no reason to doubt this.

The "downers," as he called them, were becoming more frequent and harder to pull out of. Many times he had to force himself to get out of bed in the morning, dreading having to face another day. He was worried that his grades were going to drop this semester, a real problem for a high achiever like Larry.

"Look," Larry said finally, "you know how much I love my parents and that I wouldn't hurt them for the world. But Mom and Dad, especially Dad, have forbidden me to see Angela again. And for no reason. They won't even tell me what they don't like about her. They actually say that they like her, but just don't feel she is right for me. Dr. Miller, what am I going to do? I have never faced anything like this before."

Larry was stuck on the horns of a dilemma. On one side he had twenty years of being raised in a wonderful Christian home by great parents who really loved him. On the other side was Angela, the girl he was thinking about marrying and whom he was forbidden to see.

Larry asked me to mediate between him and his parents. When I asked to see Larry's father, Bruce, I could tell he was surprised it concerned Larry and Angela. Bruce agreed to meet with me and mentioned that he thought it best that his wife, Brenda, come along for the talk.

And what a talk it was! I had not realized that Brenda was the true voice and conscience of the family, but with Bruce sitting there as though he was another of the sons, the truth of this family's dynamics was unmistakable.

I asked them both to consider what could be done to help their son, what we could share that might facilitate the family coming together again.

Brenda responded that it might help if I read a book written by a well-known "authority" on the Christian family. She also mentioned that this writer and speaker conducts seminars for Christian families, and I might better understand their position if I "had taken advantage" of them myself.

In spite of Bruce's passivity, I sensed his basic agreement with what his wife was saying. While Brenda did most of the talking, Bruce did a lot of head nodding.

I heard Brenda say that they believed children are children as long as their parents are alive and "owe" their parents obedience in all matters.

"For life?" I asked.

"For life!" was Brenda's reply.

Bruce and Brenda had apparently accepted the teachings of the seminar speaker and author, a person who had no knowledge of their family at all but who was accepted as an expert on the Brown family anyway. This person presumed to have God's blessing on telling others how they should manage their families.

I was amazed. Bruce and Brenda were educated people and solid Christians. I asked them how *they* felt about family matters, and they parroted what they had been taught in the seminars. They simply believed that God had given this stranger special abilities and insights into all families, and they trusted him implicitly.

When I pressed the issue of Larry and Angela, these parents maintained that they did not have to give their son a reason; it was Larry's "God-given" responsibility to obey them, even if they were wrong about Angela.

Even if they were wrong?

"Yes," Brenda answered, and went on to explain that they had been taught that God will bless parental decisions, even wrong decisions, as long as all family members go along. This couple wanted their twenty-year-old son to support their decision in spite of their admission that they knew they might be wrong about Angela. They proposed that if Angela was the "right kind of Christian girl," she would surrender her feelings for Larry. Brenda added that they were sure that God would curse any marriage that occurred without parental consent.

No wonder Larry was depressed. I was feeling depressed just listening to them.

There was no way Larry was going to come out of this confrontation undamaged. If he chose to try to bury his feelings for Angela, he would please his parents but go against what *he* thought God wanted him to do. If he chose to go against his parents' wishes, he would risk alienating them and possibly lose their love.

I knew the session was going to have limited benefit for Larry. Each time I tried to ask what *they* thought, I received a litany of what the "expert" had taught them. There was no willingness to consider their son's perspective. Larry was being rebellious, and that was that.

I wish I could tell you that this situation has been resolved, but to the best of my knowledge it has not. Larry and Angela are married now and have a child, but they are estranged from his parents. Larry can see his brothers only if his mom and dad don't know about it.

As I have watched this family over several years, what comes across so powerfully is their utter rejection of any kind of compromise. Whether the subject is the kind of music played in church, the sermon content, the color of the new choir robes, or the activities for young people in the Sunday school, nothing is as spiritual and "really Christian" as they would like. Bruce and Brenda are becoming increasingly legalistic, and I fully expect one day to hear that they have left their local church and now have services at home. The end of all legalism is unhappiness and dissatisfaction with everything. The combination of their own personalities and child rearing combined with the radical extra-biblical and legalistic teachings of an authority figure has finally made the Brown family dysfunctional.

Specific Costs of Legalism

Families living in legalism will experience many negatives as a result. Beyond those illustrated by the Brown family are specific impacts on individual family members. If left uncorrected they may be passed on as parenting styles to the next generation, resulting in either more excessive legalism or outright rebellion to all Christianity.

Loss of Leadership

Bruce Brown has been displaced as leader of his family, and legalism is the cause. When the dad feels his ability to lead being usurped by an authority figure, he has two choices: He may choose to resist and regain leadership, or he may quit the fight. Bruce's experience was not unique. It is a rare Christian who can garner enough spiritual fortitude to stand up against an accepted authority figure and fight for what rightly belongs to him or her.

When Bruce quit the fight, he left a leadership void in the family. Someone had to lead, and Brenda would do what Bruce would not. No faulting Brenda here; someone had to lead the family. When the father becomes less and less central in the home, the mother becomes the real power behind the throne.

If two heads really are better than one, the Brown family had lost a source of wisdom with Bruce's demotion. Brenda was willing to step in and meet the family's needs as she saw best, but from then on every decision was referred to the teachings of the seminar speaker rather than to the Bible.

Loss of Respect

Everybody loses with legalism eventually. While there are many, many short-term blessings in legalism, they are all only short term: security, fellowship, a feeling of being special as a Christian, feeling superior to less "separated" Christians, and more. But Bruce's losses were long term: respect, self-concept, power.

Brenda lost a great deal, too, though her losses may be less obvious. She also lost respect for Bruce, but what she gained in self-respect was tainted by her sense of anxiety over the long-term prospects for the family. What if other difficult problems came up with the other boys? Would she have to do it all herself? Did she sense that she had been instrumental in her husband's demotion to semifather? Much respect for themselves and each other had been sacrificed to gain the security offered by a legalistically-oriented authority figure. And respect once lost is often never regained.

Loss of Family Ties

Everyone who knows the Brown family comments that Brenda seems less happy, less content than a few years ago before their entry into legalism. Close friends admit that she seems more and more uncomfortable as head of the family, a fact no one any longer doubts. Brenda may have also lost her future relationship with children and grandchildren. What happened with Larry may happen with the other boys. No one knows for sure.

Some alienation exists between Larry and one or two of his younger brothers over his marriage to Angela. This may heal in time, but again, we can't be sure.

Loss of Confident Parenting

I wonder what Larry and his brothers think about being parents now. I can't help speculating on what the three younger boys will learn from Larry and Angela and their experience with his parents. Will the boys be stronger than the dad who surrendered his leadership to an outsider? Have they been so influenced about parenting that they, too, will seek the temporary comforts of legalism? Will they, too, turn to an "expert" when problems arise, one who knows nothing about their family?

And I am concerned about the future for Linda and Bruce. It is possible that someday one or both of these parents will come to realize that they abdicated their rights to self-respect and respect for each other to a third person or outsider. This could lead to resentment of each other or shame of themselves that in turn could result in their complete separation from each other.

Legalism Takes Its Toll

Every family touched by Christian legalism is damaged. My own family lost valuable time and experiences to the artificial limitations of a legalistic system; others will lose marriages, parent-child relationships, fellowship opportunities, and more.

This can all be avoided when we learn to trust God and take him at his word. He will not leave us or forsake us. He holds on to us, not we to him, and he cannot fail us.

The price of legalism is high, and appears to be getting higher. But we can make our families "grace-full" again and know the unconditional love and acceptance God has offered us all along. When we are in the knowledge and joy of God's grace we can pass it on to others, which is God's will for our lives.

3

Children
Legalism's Casualties

The family is designed by God to perform a specific task: to raise children to maturity in God's nurture and admonition. The function of any family is child rearing at its base, and the task of child rearing is time limited rather than open ended. Though parents usually continue to have a relationship with their grown children, the parenting aspect changes in a fundamental way once a child leaves home for the first, and usually last, time. The family exists to raise children, and to honor God in the doing.

Therefore, parents have a specific job to do and a certain amount of time to get it done. Though the basic personality is formed by the time a child begins school, the parents' influence continues for several years.

Certain parents may fear "the empty nest syndrome," but the fact is that most parents actually enjoy their new freedom and reduction in parenting responsibilities. Psychologists who study families have discovered that most parents are happier once their children are grown and on their own.

Legalism affects the family most while the children are still young, dependent upon their parents, controlled and being molded by them. Therefore, children are its main casualties. But that is not always clearly visible.

On the evening news was a most pitiful sight: a father and mother and three small children living in the family car. Gone was the security of the family home, a safe if modest income, insurance, extra money from time to time, and most of all, middle-class respectability. The father had suddenly lost his job, and with little or nothing in reserve, this young family was on the street in no time. Not really anyone's fault but maybe due to bad planning, this family was now hungry, dirty, cold, and scared. What a nightmare!

Furthermore, if the parents didn't find some way to get back to near where they were before the job was lost, they were going to lose their children, too. No, not permanently. But the state has the responsibility to see that every child in its jurisdiction is properly cared for. When parents cannot provide for the children, the state has to find someone who can.

It is a violation of moral and civil law to let a child's basic needs go unmet, regardless of the reason. No one would imagine that that young couple on the news wanted to lose their children, but that would be the result nevertheless. No matter if the concern is clothing, housing, nutrition, medical or dental care, either the parents will provide or the state will take over.

While teaching in a major city's public schools a few years ago, I noticed one of my homeroom kids coming in on a cold January morning with worn sneakers and no socks. His feet were nearly frozen, and it took the school nurse most of the morning to get his feet back in shape.

The law requires that such neglect be examined, and so it was. When the home was visited, the alcohol-addicted mother was charged with neglect, and the children were removed from her care, at least temporarily. Needless to say, the student was supplied with proper shoes and other clothing almost immediately.

Though these are extreme cases, they illustrate how seriously the government takes parenting responsibilities. Most of us would be quick to agree that the basics are critical if we want to do the right job of parenting.

In the area of physical needs, legalistic parents do an excellent job of providing for their children. What may be different when legalistic families are compared with nonlegalistic families is the decision-making process. Legalists tend to be autocratic and dictatorial in their decision making, while nonlegalistic parents tend to be closer to the democratic end of the spectrum. But legalistic parents generally do take very good physical care of their children, considering it to be immoral to fail on such serious responsibilities.

Family Responsibility and Accountability

Division of responsibility and approaches to accountability are important in all families. More than who does what and when, the more basic philosophy is under consideration here, and it is here that we begin to see some major differences between legalistic and nonlegalistic Christian families.

As legalistic Christian parents are both authoritarian and autocratic, household duties are likely to be assigned by one parent and will be based on that one parent's own preferences as to what males and females and the different ages may or may not do.

Many legalistic Christian families develop a form of papacy related to anything remotely resembling a spiritual decision. Healthy families tend to be more lighthearted and flexible about relationships with one another. Unhealthy legalistic families tend to be headed by a father who sees his role as that of an all-powerful authority who must make all-important decisions alone. Legalistic families tend to be more tied to tradition, because tradition means safety, and safety is all-important to the legalist.

The same papal mind-set applies to accountability. When a decision is right, Dad gets the credit. When the decision is wrong, Dad bears the guilt.

Where is Mom? In a great number of legalistic Christian families, Mom is the oldest child, an adult with no "voting privileges" and no "rights." The inherent weakness in such a system should be apparent. First, when the father dies, becomes too ill to work, or is otherwise disabled a family or its individual members do not have the inner strength or benefit of experience to carry on.

Such fathers are also at risk. I have seen them sink into depression the likes of which few secular counselors see outside a mental hospital. If Dad is accountable and responsible for everything, he will eventually feel the pain of being a spiritual island, Mom being a second-class Christian (female, you know) and really unable (in Dad's mind) to be of much help. Such marriages are weaker than anyone would imagine just looking at externals.

Socializing and Civilizing: The Difference

Parents are accountable for the underlying attitudes and philosophies of life they transmit to their children. These often are not consciously expressed by words or overt actions and are more difficult for parents to recognize, but they are powerful.

Linda and I grew up in and around Detroit. Learning to drive in a city like Detroit means learning self-preservation along with parallel parking. Part of self-preservation is being able to let other drivers know what you think of their driving skills. All fair, we were taught, because they will surely let you know what they think.

All of Linda's relatives lived in Cleveland, about a three-hour trip on the Ohio Turnpike. One Saturday morning on one of our many trips to visit the Cleveland side of the family we had seven-year-old Laurie, four-year-old Doug, and baby Jennifer along.

As we were tooling down the turnpike, some idiot pulled in front of us at sixty miles an hour. Practicing my Detroit driver education skills I shouted, "You idiot! Why don't you watch where you're going?" A rhetorical question at best; the other driver couldn't hear me, after all. But I surely felt good, at least for a few minutes.

The next time a car pulled in front of us, both Laurie and Doug shouted in unison, "You idiot! Why don't you watch where you're going?" And if that wasn't bad enough, they turned to me and smiled, obviously waiting for me to tell them what a great job they had done in protecting the Miller family automobile.

Linda looked over at me, and as only a wife can, *suggested* we have a lesson on proper language addressed to strangers, even strangers in cars who can't hear us.

We had the lesson, with me serving as both student and teacher. I was struck by how much I had been teaching without meaning to.

But let us get back to the children and the deeper philosophical implications of legalism that can affect them. Not all children will be affected or respond in the same way, of course, but I believe all children of legalistic families are damaged to some degree. In the two examples that follow, one child passively absorbed a legalistic philosophy only to become socially stunted; in the other example the children struck back.

First it is necessary to distinguish between what it means to civilize children and to socialize them. To civilize children is to teach them correct behavior for a variety of situations. To be civil means to behave in an appropriate, courteous, and considerate manner.

To socialize children is to prepare them for person-to-person interaction. To be socialized is to be one step above being civilized. It means being capable of conducting normal, friendly, nonoffensive interactions with people from many different backgrounds and perspectives. A socialized person is comfortable with people from different backgrounds and who may hold radically different religious beliefs, and has the skills to share his or her faith in a manner that leaves others feeling friendly toward that person even if they reject the religious position. To be socialized is to have empathy for people as different as possible while still sensitive to their worldviews and perspectives on life and death.

Being socialized means loving people anyway.

I must digress here to explain that the idea of being socialized has nothing to do with the political-economic system of socialism. Lest this appears to be a ridiculous statement, I offer the following anecdote.

As Linda and I were getting the kids ready for the start of another school year, we were particularly excited because our oldest, Laurie, was beginning seventh grade. And was she excited!

I dropped the kids off at their respective schools and noticed that the social studies department of the junior high school had changed its name to heritage studies.

Heritage studies?

You will remember that one of my weaknesses was asking "stupid" questions, and this was going to be no exception. So I asked.

"Well," the principal sighed, "apparently someone objected to the concept of anything 'social' being taught here, and because we wouldn't want to offend anyone, the leadership [obviously not including the principal] decided to just go ahead and change the name."

"Social" might offend someone? Then it dawned on me. Legalists are frightened people, remember, and those were the days when socialism meant communism—one of Christian legalism's most feared and targeted enemies.

It was never explained why those who might be "offended" could not be educated as to the true nature of social studies. Being a former social studies teacher I almost snickered as I wondered if the teachers would now have to call themselves heritage studies teachers. The worries of legalism had caused this very large, influential Christian university and day school to risk other educators' ridicule just because someone might misunderstand.

The best people among us are both civil and social. Legalistic parents generally do an excellent job of civilizing their children. Visit any legalistic day school or college and you will come away impressed with the well-behaved, carefully dressed young people there. Children in legalistic churches frequently are not permitted in the main sanctuary, but they would be well behaved if they were there. I recall an entire chapel service devoted to the morality of picking up dropped tissues from the ground and the sin of dropping the tissues in the first place.

The reason for this good behavior might be nothing more than an intense fear of getting into trouble. Of course, there are well-behaved youngsters who really want to be good, but some wise and knowledgeable people do wonder whether any children raised in a legalistic system can be completely well.

Poorly Socialized

I needed a summer job to supplement my teaching salary at the college one year and was happy to find an opening on the paint crew. I have always enjoyed painting, and the change of pace from teaching was refreshing. It was during this summer that I met Barry.

Barry was the son of missionaries and a junior at the college. He was unable to go home that summer, and so we found ourselves on the same crew. We spent many hours together that summer scraping, sanding, and painting all manner of school rooms, campus houses, even furniture.

One morning Barry mentioned that he was trying to sell his car. He needed the money to pay off his school bill before he could enroll for the fall semester. He placed an ad in the paper and was happy a man was interested in his car.

A few days later Barry announced that he thought he had a deal on the car, and was he ever relieved!

But then things fell apart. The man changed his mind at the last minute, and Barry was not going to sell his car. At least not right then.

Barry was distraught. Then he made the comment that has stayed with me all these years and which so clearly illustrates the legalistic Christian mind-set.

"I guess I should have expected this," Barry said. "When Christians deal with the world we have to expect to get beat up."

Christians should expect to be losers in the world? What an outlook on life!

This Christian young man not only had failed to sell his car. What happened was much more serious, complicated, and even spiritual. Barry the good person had been abused by a bad person, and wasn't he dumb to have expected anything else!

Barry was a civilized young man—polite to a fault, courteous, well spoken, tactful, and careful not to offend anyone. But Barry was very poorly socialized—suspicious, distrustful, arrogant, and quick to blame others.

I do not know what became of Barry. I know that he did graduate and get married and is out in the world he feared, undoubtedly trying his best to please God and the authority figures who replaced the university he once attended. He is out there somewhere, likely raising children to be as suspicious and negative about people as he is. I doubt if these words of Jesus have yet found a place in Barry's suspicious heart: "Behold, I send you forth as sheep in the midst of wolves; be ye therefore wise as serpents, and harmless as doves" (Matt. 10:16). God sent Barry as he sends each of us into the midst of wolves, expecting that we learn something of the ways of wolves. Barry had learned how to be a sheep, but he had failed to learn about wolves.

Striking Back

As was shown in the previous chapter, Christian families led by legalistic parents can be expected to take the position that children are children as long as parents are alive. Parental authority, legalists believe, does not terminate with grown children leaving home and starting their own families. Those parents admit that things change and that parental power is diminished, but it is still there.

There are advantages to this kind of continuing involvement. Grown children generally feel much support and security from their parents. They are sure of their parents' willingness to step in and help in emergencies, which might be more quickly expressed than in nonlegalistic families. The downside, though, is that this willingness to help is often conditional, dependent on the conformity of grown children to do what parents expect.

The following story took place in a solid, Bible-believing, Bible-preaching church.

The pastor and his wife were parents to two boys. Though the home was strict even by legalistic standards (the need to set examples to the church) both boys seemed well adjusted, happy, and solidly Christian.

But looks can be deceiving.

James, the younger son, felt called by God into the preaching ministry and had recently graduated from a conservative seminary. Cliff, the older son by three years, had "defied" (a common term in legalistic families) his father's desire, which he was sure was the Spirit's calling, that Cliff also become a minister. But Cliff had gone into the construction business after graduating from a Christian college with a business degree. (As an aside, one of the characteristics that distinguishes legalistic Christians from others is their belief that there is but one "really good, really biblical" Christian college, probably the one the parents attended, or the pastor.)

I knew that the pastor was a strong supporter of the leader of seminars on the Christian family mentioned earlier. That speaker was accepted by the pastor and deacons as an unquestioned authority on all matters relevant to the family. He it was who pushed the idea that children remain under parental authority as long as parents are alive, calling it the chain of command.

Cliff was not excited about the chain of command, no matter what his parents thought. Cliff had made his decision to go into business rather than answer that call of God that only his father could hear. Cliff's parents were convinced that the message they had received from the Holy Spirit about Cliff's life took precedence over what Cliff believed God wanted him to do.

It came as quite a surprise to the church when the pastor announced that one of his sons had "disgraced the church" by leaving his wife and admitting to plans to marry someone else. The shock was magnified, however, when it was revealed that the wayward son was James and not Cliff.

Cliff had openly asserted his independence from legalism's grip. But when James broke free he struck back with sad and sinful results. Those who know the pastor and his family say he never seemed to be the same after that announcement. A few years later he and his wife quietly retired and moved away. Friends said the pastor had lost his power that day.

The question remains whether this tragedy should have been as destructive as it turned out to be. It is easy to speculate on the role of legalism in this situation and the damage done by the extra-biblical teachings of an authority figure leading family seminars.

There is clearly a release point in every life when parents are left behind and an individual and separate life begun. Legalistic parents resist allowing the Holy Spirit to lead their grown children in directions different from what they have in mind. But the Bible clearly states there is a point when a person is *required* to leave mother and father. Jesus said: "For this cause shall a man leave father and mother, and shall cleave to his wife, and they two shall be one flesh" (Matt. 19:5).

Legalism and Family Function

Family function relates to the day-to-day work of being in a family. For parents this means providing a sense of order and a feeling of accomplishment for family members. Becoming both civilized and socialized are included in family function as are the needs for discipline and love.

This is a tall order for two ordinary people who are only temporarily parents. The task is made easier for those who themselves received high quality parenting as they grew up and experience the continuing influence of their parents even in their adult independence. No one denies that people basically parent as they were parented, for good or bad. How, then, is family function affected by legalism?

Legalism provides both safety and restriction for a family. Safety is in being completely accepted as long as a member stays within the boundaries established by the family's authority figure. Restrictions exist because of those very boundaries, with outward conformity taking on disproportionate and stifling importance.

At one of the Christian universities where I taught, it was not unusual for faculty members to be reminded of the "school position" on certain matters. Those matters would not seem the least bit controversial to someone outside legalism, as would abortion, social drinking, women in the pastorate, or inerrancy of Scripture. (These were clear cut and not even considered for debate, not at *this* legalistic school.)

No, we were cautioned about teaching the benefits of group learning as against individual learning. We were warned about the "hidden messages" college students might learn by allowing "too much" class discussion. I was in hot water on one occasion for asking for a room with movable chairs so I could teach group counseling skills to a *graduate* counseling class.

My request was refused.

When faculty asked about these limitations, the appropriate dean would remind the faculty member that "we need to all speak with one voice" at this university, which really meant all faculty must support the administration's position.

Families can become like this, too. Any divergence from "the party (family) line" automatically puts that family member in the position of being wrong, or even malicious. Legalists have little time for personal opinions, unless they are the opinions of authority figures. Having all one's ducks in a row may present a picture of a well-run family, but such conformity belies the turmoil building slowly as the children grow into adolescence.

This conformity applies equally to rules. When legalists proclaim that "God is not a God of disorder," children and other "subordinates" had better watch out for a new rule or regulation about to be handed down. Christian legalism produces well-behaved children, but the good behavior reflects this strong underlying philosophy: *Rules exist to keep the children from doing bad, not to encourage them to do good.* This is another manifestation of the negative mindset so typical of legalistic Christians.

In legalistic and well-behaved families, having a messy room is not just being sloppy or careless but a sin and a comment on one's character. Having a dirty car is not simply having a car that needs washing but a bad testimony. The faculty members of a legalistic Christian university were once told that they were guilty of sin if they failed to get their automobiles registered on time.

Legalists' children learn that what they look like is at least as important, and maybe more important, than what they are on the inside. Put another way, *legalism teaches Christian living as a performance art for the benefit of those who may be watching.*

This need for order and control of the way things look, typical of legalistic families, extends even to emotional and sexual issues—not the big questionable issues but the mere hugs and kisses between family members most people would see as normal expressions of affection. Because legalistic Christian families are very "others conscious," they tend to avoid expressions of affection for fear they will be misunderstood.

The obvious danger here is that children may develop a warped attitude about any form of emotional expression. I have done enough family counseling with Christians to know that this is a very real possibility. Boys and girls are taught that emotions, like sex, are to be feared and kept under control at all costs. Those who counsel Christians acknowledge that a great deal of the trouble can be traced to their childhood lessons in the repression of honest emotion.

It does not take too much stretch of the imagination to see that children growing up in such an atmosphere can develop low estimates of their worth as individuals and unhealthy guilt that burdens them well into adulthood. The ultimate tragedy is that such individuals are then unable to fully accept the unconditional love of God.

4

Legalistic
and Nonlegalistic
Families
How They Differ

Every Christian has a responsibility to know all there is to know about the difference between well-functioning and dysfunctional families.

Every Christian must know, not only counselors and therapists but all people who extend Christian help to others. This responsibility is not limited to pastors and evangelists, for much of the good that happens to Christian families is a result of their being discipled by lay Christians. And there is no age limitation on the need to know. Grandparents can be the most powerful force this side of God when it comes to influencing grandchildren to follow God's direction for their lives.

What distinguishes good Christian families from dysfunctional Christian families? Specific areas to look at are family communication, interpersonal relationships within the family, power structure and application, emotional expression, and coping ability. These will help us to analyze our own families and families who need help.

I believe that *all* legalistic families are dysfunctional. Certainly good qualities are to be found in legalistic families, but it is the core of the family we are concerned with, not how the family "looks." My training and experience in family counseling, plus the years my family spent deep in legalism, have provided insights leading me to this conclusion.

Furthermore, I firmly believe there are striking similarities between legalistic families and cultic families. The mind-sets are identical: reliance on a single authority figure, the perspective that the individual exists to serve the group, and the submission to authoritarian leadership. The major difference that keeps Christian legalistic families from becoming truly cultic is their acceptance of the basic doctrines of Christianity, including the deity of Jesus Christ, but the danger to individuals in such families exists despite this one saving difference.

It is encouraging to see how many families are breaking free of legalism and experiencing the liberty and unconditional love God intended all along. Therefore, we should not be pessimistic but become more determined than ever to help others do the same.

Communication Patterns: Legalistic Families

For one of my first counseling experiences I was asked to see Mr. and Mrs. Jacobson, who were concerned with some problems in their marriage. The Jacobsons were a respected family in the community and were members of a hyperstrict, legalistic, area church. The couple asked if they could bring their fourteen-year-old daughter JoAnne with them, because as an only child she was intimately involved with what had been going on at home. I agreed, because this was their first session and I thought it might be helpful to get a sense of how this trio dealt with each other.

I greeted the family in the waiting room of the counseling center and escorted them back to my office where we could talk. My office had unusually thin walls and virtually no soundproofing to protect the people in the other offices. But shouting was not something that normally happened in my office.

They settled into their chairs, JoAnne sitting between her mom and dad, and the first skirmish began almost immediately.

Mrs. J. delivered a broadside to Mr. J. about his lack of backbone. He shot back with a cooking criticism. Back and forth, back and forth, their shouting became louder and louder with each volley of shots. JoAnne was in the middle trying to wave a truce flag but being ignored.

I had never seen a couple move so quickly into combat, and while in a "neutral" zone, too. It amounted to lots of talk, lots of noise, multiplied accusations and recriminations, but no communication. What I was observing was all talk and no listening.

I was finally able to settle them down, and we began to work on their concerns, but I was so impressed with how little in the way of communication had gone on. It also became clear that this family was distinctly legalistic. When such families talk with each other, the interchanges are typically vague, confused, accusatory, and avoidant, particularly noticeable when things are going badly for them.

Parents who are made to feel incompetent in their parenting react with communication patterns reflecting those negative feelings about themselves. Furthermore, legalism teaches parents to cover problems over so "the cause of Christ" won't be hindered, leading to a "pressure cooker" process culminating in the kind of explosion I witnessed with the Jacobsons in my office.

The dynamics of these communication problems are not difficult to understand within the framework of legalism. Legalism teaches, directly or indirectly, that being vague is a good way to stay out of trouble. Its adherents are reluctant to take positions for fear of being criticized or punished should their opinions be wrong. The fear of criticism is usually so strong in legalistic families that everyone other than the authority figure sees value in measuring words very carefully, and if keeping quiet is impossible, to speak in vague generalities so as not to be pinned down in criticism. This is what I observed in the Jacobson family.

Confusion is more typical in younger children who are just beginning to learn the rules of family legalism. Older children and the nondominant parent have learned by experience which subjects are likely to cause the dominant parent to become upset and how to avoid being drawn into a controversy. But the younger kids are in for a hard time until they catch on.

Along with evasive types of communication a double-bind type of interaction creeps in. A double-bind message is one that is difficult to understand, because the words of the speaker do not match the body language, facial expressions, or tone of voice. Who could forget a childhood experience of trouble with a parent followed by a sincere if fearful apology, followed by an exclamation by the parent, "All right, that's enough! I said it's okay and I don't want to hear any more about it. Understand?" Obviously, such a parent is still upset, no matter what he says about forgiving.

Double-bind messages result from a psychological process known as compensation. This process stems from the parent's need to express love and care for a child, but is compensated by another side that says parents are supposed to be judges and critics of their children.

"Yes Billy, I'm really happy with the B you earned in math class."

Pause.

"But we both know you could have done better, don't we?"

Nine-year-old Billy thinks, *Mom said she was happy with my B in math. But if she is really happy, why would she suggest that I didn't work as hard as I could? Should I be pleased with myself for the B, or not?*

Many adults have acquired the idea, often from their own parents, that compliments to children must always be conditional or they will get all "puffed up"—egotistical—and will become lazy in the future. Maybe Billy's mom really was happy with that B in math but had learned that good parents always balance a compliment with a criticism—to keep the child's ego in balance, you see. Unfortunately, this overlooks the child's feelings.

Legalistic families also are prone to what psychologists call nonreciprocal communication. This is a powerful factor resulting from the parents' belief that whatever may be contributed by children and teens in the family is not worthy of consideration. Parents who see their roles as leaders, directors, and controllers of the young in the family naturally progress to where communication is one way only: parent to child.

Communication in legalistic families has been described by some as militaristic in the sense that certain people may talk to certain members but not to others. Children and teens who are allowed to contribute very little to a family discussion grow up feeling left out and unimportant, outside the "power loop" of the family.

Not only youngsters can feel left out of the decision-making process; often wives do, too. Many families in legalistic churches are led by husbands who have been taught that spiritual leadership means that they *alone* must make the final decisions, spiritual or not. In such marriages the two who are one are not really partners.

Communication Patterns: Nonlegalistic Families

Changing communication patterns is very difficult. But as I have said, there is hope for recovery for legalists, and healing is based in large part on becoming aware of what really good communication is.

Nonlegalistic Christian families express themselves clearly, openly, and spontaneously. Clarity, openness, and spontaneity are indispensable in giving children the freedom to do "trial and error" communication when they are very young. By contrast, research demonstrates that young people in trouble with the law typically come from families distinctive for their failure to communicate effectively with each other.

For example, a large group of juvenile delinquents were interviewed and asked questions about the rules their parents imposed at home. Using curfew as an example, delinquent young people said that they had rules for what time to be in the house, but when pressed for details, these kids had a hard time coming up with specifics, such as exact times on weeknights, weekends, holidays, or during summers. These same youngsters said there were obviously things they could not do at home; on the other hand there were many exceptions and special times when the rules might not apply, such as when parents were feeling especially good, paydays, and maybe birthdays. While legalistic families have clearly stated rules, the rules are not so clearly understood, leading to strictly enforced behavior, but confusion about why something is right or wrong.

By comparison, when a similar group of young people not in trouble with the law were interviewed, they were able to give exact details of rules and regulations at home and specify the few times there were exceptions. They experienced clearly communicated and understood rules and were much the better off for it.

Another distinction between legalistic and nonlegalistic Christian families is reciprocity and honesty in communication. Not only is everyone in the nonlegalistic family allowed to talk to anyone else, but they are actually encouraged to do so. The subject of acceptable conversation is more open and honest than in legalistic families. This reciprocity and honesty conveys the message to young people in the family that while their parents may not agree with what they say or ask for, they are free to say what they want to say or ask for without being criticized or punished for talking.

Nonlegalistic families are able to joke with and tease one another in good spirit. Healthy families can laugh at their own and others' pratfalls without feelings being hurt. Each member has enough personal security within the family structure to be able to relax and have fun.

Listening to the way family members speak with one another makes it possible to diagnose a legalistic family without knowing very much else about that family.

Relationships: Legalistic Families

This is how one twelve-year-old boy answered me when I asked him to tell me something about his father. He smiled when he used the word, but there was pain in his voice that was unmistakable: "tyrannosaurus dad."

I wonder how many fathers would be willing to have *that* written as their epitaph?

Like a skyscraper, family patterns are built on a foundation that is mostly unseen buried beneath the surface and covered over with years of personal and family history. What actually happens in a family is what we can see from the outside, above the surface. What is seen is often less important than what is not seen, though.

Layers are added with each new child born into the family and with every person's birthday in the family, parents' included. The concept of layering may help to understand how relationships evolve in legalistic Christian families. The legalistic family may not actually enjoy the strict, tense, fearful atmosphere at home, but if it is all either parent has ever known, it is certain to be repeated. What they do may be nothing more sinister than a reflection of the only parenting practices the parents were ever exposed to. However, we can find hope here. What has been learned can always be unlearned, and with years of practice change, though difficult, is never, never impossible.

Tyrannosaurus dad was an exaggeration, of course, but the man's characteristics that made his son give him that label were unquestionably acquired at the feet of his own father, *his* tyrannosaurus dad.

Relationship patterns in legalistic families are characterized by ambivalence and uncertainty based on members' underlying need to conform. If then an absolute standard of behavior eludes them, family interactions will shift from criticism to expressions of love and support; from a judgmental attitude to occasional periods of openness and unconditional acceptance. Researchers tell us that legalistic parents will eventually acknowledge the need for change, perhaps based on nothing more than family unhappiness.

This ambivalence carries over from personal uncertainty to child rearing practices and manifests itself in parental inconsistency in discipline and daily interaction patterns. The common complaint I hear from grown children of legalistic Christian parents is that the discipline inflicted on them as children was both harsh and inflexible. Other descriptions of legalistic family discipline include unfair, failure to consider circumstances, and extreme. Inconsistency stems from one or both parents' feeling that maybe they were too tough during discipline, causing a temporary "lightening up," followed eventually by a reminder from an authority figure to avoid leniency lest the kids become punk rockers or drug addicts, then a return to being harsh, until guilt creeps in once again telling parents to lighten up.

I have found that legalistic Christian parents who experience these fluctuating bouts of inconsistency are usually closer to accepting help for their family than those who manage to be more unbending. Inconsistency always reflects uncertainty, and uncertainty is fertile ground for healing. We need to remember that growth comes only from discomfort with the status quo.

Husband-wife relationships are also colored by legalism. Any relationship that has criticism and judgment as a part of its foundation is bound to crumble at some point. The presence of marital discord is the gas beneath the surface just waiting to explode, as it did with the Jacobsons.

Legalistic Christian wives initially try to divert their concern over their marriages into concern for one or more of the children. This usually surfaces only after several counseling sessions discussing the "presenting problem" of a fourth grader who just won't do his homework or a teenager who refuses to take out the rubbish. Once the wife feels she can trust the counselor, the truth begins to flow.

Legalistic Christian men, on the other hand, are almost universally resistant to seeing a counselor for any reason.

Such men have an impossibly difficult time admitting that there is a problem at home they are unable to deal with satisfactorily. The teachings of legalism built up over many years encrust men with a hard shell protecting sensitive feelings. The hope is that when husbands and fathers see the very real danger of losing wife and family to separation and divorce, a new willingness to face up to family issues can lead to a much improved family condition. But that often is a tenuous hope.

Relationships: Nonlegalistic Families

Nonlegalistic Christian families tend to be characterized by members' desires to spend time with one another. Joy in doing things together is reflected in all aspects of the family's being, and produces trust, encouragement, and a nonpossessive need to be in contact with one another.

Nonlegalistic families tend to express an honest acceptance of the differences between family members. They will not tend to equate a member's need for solitude with rejection of the others, as often happens in legalistic families. Less legalistic Christian dads are typically more willing to admit their failures and accept pastoral or other help. They have a healthy recognition that failures will occur and that such failures are really opportunities for learning.

Nonlegalistic families demonstrate warmth and caring for one another. Parents express mutual satisfaction with the state of their marriage, recognizing that imperfections do not equal failure. Their care for each other is shown by their willingness to share household chores and caring for the children. Show me a legalistic Christian husband and father and I will show you a man who, even if his wife works full time outside the home, insists on the privilege of being a "couch potato" when he gets home from work.

Shared responsibility is important to the health of any family, Christian or not. Children learn that sharing duties is no threat to anyone's personhood. When Mom catches the flu, Dad can step in and do all that needs doing, not as well perhaps, but his "male ego" is not threatened by doing dishes or changing a diaper. Similarly if Dad is ill or injured, Mom can step in and replace a fuse or mow the yard without feeling less feminine for doing so.

A fine Christian lady told me one day that the real reason she was so reluctant to drive long distances by herself was that she had never pumped gas into the car herself and didn't even know how to get the gas cap off. Such handicapping makes everyone losers in a legalistic family with a strict division-of-labor philosophy.

In the Miller household Linda and I agreed early that our children would not be disadvantaged by what we saw as unfair attitudes about the division of labor. We made a conscious effort to train ourselves in the tasks typically done by each other. Linda knows how to start a lawn-mower and I have done laundry, grocery shopping, and rinsed out dirty diapers. (It is amazing how "spiritual" the most ungodly man can get when it comes time to explain to his wife why it is not "appropriate" for him to change a diaper. "God never intended men to wash dishes" comes the pious response to a request for help, as if God cared at all who does the dishes!) We really believe our kids are healthier for being exposed to parents who did not divide their duties along sexual lines.

Power Structure: Legalistic Families

Power corrupts, the saying goes, and absolute power corrupts absolutely.

We all know about the president of Universal Motors who is reported to treat his "underlings" like dirt, or the

Wall Street shark who was once power and money crazy and because of stock manipulation now sits in a minimum security prison in Alabama making pot holders.

We wonder about the power exerted by pastors and their staffs, television preachers, and yes, even Mother Teresa comes under suspicion for having some kind of a "hidden power agenda."

We really do wonder about such people, don't we? But us? What kind of power abuse can an assistant manager of a department store or an appliance repairman exert? People like us work for *everybody!* Whom could we, even if we were legalistic Christians, abuse with power?

The only targets of power abuse in most lives are family members, primarily wives and children. Especially in legalistic Christian families do we see such a fertile field just waiting to be planted with the dangerous seeds of power and exploitation.

But not only in legalistic Christian families.

In any situation involving human beings and an unequal distribution of power, corruption is a possibility. We see this all over the world and especially in the recent collapse of communist regimes in Eastern Europe. What we have seen in Romania, Panama, the Philippines, and many other nations should not surprise us. But that we should see a scaled down but similar abuse of power in Christian families is not to be so expected. However, what despots around the world have done to their nations with their illegally acquired power, many legalistic Christian parents have done with the authority they received from God.

Legalistic Christian families are likely to be father dominated. His control extends to virtually every aspect of life and is not limited to spiritual concerns. Mom is not regarded as a partner but as a subordinate. This dominant/inferior relationship is in opposition to what God teaches about genuine love in a family and results in a life filled not only with submission by a wife and children but resentment and bitterness, too.

We know that physical and sexual abuse of children is more likely to occur in legalistic homes. Not only Protestant Christian, but Roman Catholic, Mormon, Moslem, or any religion that can be taken to an extreme is fertile ground for such problems.

The quiet truth known to Christian counselors and pastors is that the stricter and more legalistic the family, the greater the risk of one of these awful forms of child abuse. This is not to say that legalistic families cannot be morally responsible; many are never at risk for such abuse. But the general risk is there, nevertheless.

Abuse of power, perceived threats to power, or a need to assert a shaky sense of power can drive a man into this generally well-kept secret.

Hard evidence and firm statistics are difficult to find, but those of us who work with Christian families know that our caseload involving Christian families and some form of abuse is increasing rapidly.

Counseling can help, but only if parents, especially fathers, are willing to discuss family concerns with a Christian counselor. As was said earlier, legalistic fathers are resistant to talking to anyone about family matters—resistant, that is, until something terrible happens and they are forced to undergo counseling by child protective services. A Christian counselor should be carefully chosen to avoid legalistic attitudes. Parents can ask about attitudes on separation, equal status in the family, and dealing with authority figures to assess the counselor's position on legalism.

One final observation on power is that because legalists cannot support the more extreme aspects of family regulations with biblical or scientific research evidence, they tend to be sensitive to the slightest challenge or apparent criticism. Legalists seldom or never respond to challenges to their power or its basis in terms of content or accuracy. Rather, challenges are met with proclamations of "creeping liberalism" or some such thing, not worthy of comment. If this tactic fails, legalists will turn next to ridicule, a risky move at best considering the truth in the axiom that "ridicule is the last defense of a weak mind."

When a family sees its leader resorting to ridicule rather than rationality to resolve a challenge, the children and young people sense the inherent weakness in what they are witnessing. Instead of toughening up the family to fight off "liberalism," ridicule convinces the youngsters that parents and authority figures have been wrong in the stand they have taken. I recall sitting in a chapel service at the large Christian legalistic university where I taught listening to its president ridicule another Christian university. As we walked out of the service, I overheard one student say to another, "Boy, they must have something pretty good up there the way the president was making fun of them."

As Abraham Lincoln said, "You cannot fool all of the people all of the time."

Power Structure: Nonlegalistic Families

The predominant feeling in nonlegalistic Christian families is one of basic equality of merit, if not of position. For example, nonlegalistic fathers typically acknowledge in both words and actions that parents are equal—different in function but equal in the eyes of God. Children are not equal, not yet, because they are still dependents who need nurturing. But someday they will be on equal footing with their parents, honoring them because they want to rather than because they have to.

Nonlegalistic Christian families are characterized by true shared power in the home, flexibility in decision making, and a willingness to consider the viewpoints of the children. This kind of respect does not mean that the family should be a democratic, one-person, one-vote organization. But it does mean that parents will listen to and consider what the kids have to say.

When Linda and I learned that we would be leaving the Christian university in the spring after having ministered there six years, we were a little concerned about how the children would take the news. Our children were then sixteen, thirteen, and about ten. Laurie, our oldest would be graduating from the campus high school before we would move and we thought she would take the news the best. We were unsure of how the younger two would feel about moving away.

So we prayed about how to tell them.

We called them into the living room one evening after dinner and told them that, for many reasons, we would not be returning to the next school year. We were pleasantly surprised when they all agreed that moving might not be so terrible after all, and we discussed our possibilities as we saw them then. We had a pretty good time that evening speculating on the pros and cons of the various options. Linda and I asked the kids to tell us where they would most like to move if they could choose. We discussed that the family would follow God's leading on this, but we would consider their wishes if at all possible. The children knew that we cared about their opinions even though in the end we could not move to where they wished.

Because legalistic parents have been taught that authority is unapproachable, they tend to be less approachable as parents. Equality is a sign of weakness to legalists. They believe that God is an authoritarian manipulator who will do what is best for them whether they like it or not and they approach their parenting in the same way.

But if we believe we have a God who wants to give us what we ask for as long as it is good for us and that he has no desire to manipulate us against our will, we parents will tend to have the same attitude about children, the "inferior" members of the family. To the same extent that legalism is limiting, nonlegalism is liberating.

The Power of Early Experiences: The Story of Jacob

Good family feelings lead to a solid sense of self worth in youngsters that is in outstanding contrast to the self-doubt and feelings of guilt so typical of children in legalistic families. If parents can really understand that they are in fact the first "gods" their children will know, they should also be able to raise their level of sensitivity regarding the accidental and hidden messages they send their kids when they are small. It is easy to move from this point to understanding how a super-strict, critical, authoritarian, "tyrannosaurus dad" might push a small child away from God.

Feeling emotionally safe in a family is the first step in coming to accept the love of God and a personal relationship with Jesus Christ. The following story illustrates this.

We met Jacob and Marilyn when they visited our "young marrieds" Sunday school class. As new Christians, Linda and I were interested in getting to know others like ourselves, and the Millers and Arbitours quickly became friends. We learned that Jacob was raised in upper New York State by parents who adopted him when he was about four years old. Marilyn confided to Linda that her husband had serious problems dealing with rejection and struggled with very low self-esteem. He was sensitive to any comment that could be remotely critical and was not able to take even the slightest teasing.

During one of the Wednesday evening prayer services at the church, our pastor was continuing a study of the love of God. Linda and I noticed that Jacob became visibly agitated when the idea of God the Father was mentioned.

After three weeks of lessons on this subject, Jacob suddenly stood to his feet in the middle of the message and shouted, "Listen, people, what I want to know is where is *my* father? What I want to know is if God loves me so much, how come he gave me parents who abandoned me?"

Jacob seemed to all of a sudden realize what he had done and quickly sat down, quietly weeping. Marilyn went to the ladies' room, while George, our Sunday school teacher took Jacob outside the room to counsel with him.

We never saw this couple again. We were told that they eventually divorced after having changed churches several times. Marilyn told a mutual friend that her husband's self-concept had gotten so low that he was impossible to live with.

This young man was so badly damaged by his first four years of life that he was not able (as far as we know) to overcome his feeling of being rejected. The important feeling of security in a family had passed Jacob by in those early years, permanently limiting his ability to understand the true meaning of God's unconditional love for him. He could not believe that his heavenly father would do for him what his earthly Father had not.

Emotional Expression: Legalistic Families

Legalistic Christians commonly shy away from doing or saying anything that might lead others to believe that they are not as traditional or conservative as they ought to be.

It makes sense that this concern with what others think would teach the value of keeping emotional expressions in check until the environment proves itself safe for emotional expression of some sort. Legalistic Christians take the positions taught them by their own authority figures in the church. Just as some Christians refer questions about personal religious beliefs to "whatever my church believes," when it comes to expressing happiness, anger, outrage, joy, and sorrow, legalists check for prevailing winds.

The fear of being misunderstood coupled with a need to check out everything with others leads legalistic Christians to emotional expressions that are cynical, often hostile, and even malicious. A legalistic Christian pastor loves no joke more than one about "the opposition." I don't mean the devil here, but the cross-town rival church that doesn't conform to proper legalistic practices.

One thing is very sure. Never, under any circumstances short of a proven moral failure, will the congregation in a legalistic church rise to challenge its authority figure. The "monsters" of this discussion exist only because the teachings of legalism have made it so very difficult to challenge *any* authority figure, even such a leader deep in moral sin.

Emotional Expression: Nonlegalistic Families

But the coin of emotional expression has a nonlegalistic side, the side used by Christians who can be spontaneous and have fun without worrying what others might think about them.

I once served as a camp counselor at a Christian summer camp. This was a large and well-known camp supported by several larger churches in the state, all of whom were of the "fundamentalist, super-separated, legalistic" variety.

The camp skit and what we all learned

The kids in each camp area had an opportunity to develop a "skit" for the entertainment of the other campers. The group I was working with decided to present a show based on the guest speaker himself. This well-known evangelist was famous for having big feet, something on the order of size thirteen on a man only five feet nine inches tall.

So the kids thought it would be amusing to get one of the kids in the skit to dress up in a suit and put on the biggest shoes he could find in camp.

Sure enough, the skit went on and the shoes flopped across the stage to roars from the audience. I laughed more than anyone, because I had heard my own pastor kid this same speaker to his face about the size of his feet, and more than once.

I noticed that the evangelist wasn't laughing, and neither was the camp director.

Later that evening we were visited in our cabin by the director and the evangelist. We were roundly "chewed out" for being disrespectful to this "man of God," and even though there was nothing unkind or un-Christian in the skit, we all felt pretty guilty.

The more I thought about it the more I was bothered that the kids I was responsible for might get the idea that it is okay to kid "ordinary" Christians, but authority figures are sacred and off limits. When I asked the camp director about my concerns, I was reminded forcefully that "we can't do anything to detract from a Christian leader's ability to minister and lead," though how the big-shoes skit put his ministry at risk was never explained.

Note also that the evangelist was standing right there allowing himself to be portrayed by the director as too sacred for a little good-natured kidding. What a different impression of Christian authority would have been presented to these boys by a humble Christian evangelist who did not see himself as too big to be kidded and too holy for humor.

There is a night and day difference in the way legalistic and nonlegalistic Christians express their emotions. Emotions are to be controlled and kept under, according to legalism, feared, and avoided, and always carefully evaluated before being expressed.

But nonlegalistic Christians can take jokes, even when they are the targets, and show genuine warmth and caring for others, even if one of them is wearing big floppy shoes.

Coping Ability: Legalistic Families

The ability of a Christian family to cope with problems is our final area of discussion and one that serves well to summarize and highlight the important differences between legalistic and nonlegalistic families.

Because of legalists' emphasis on tradition and valuing the way things have always been done, change is threatening by its very possibility, not only in regard to the undesirable changes taking place in society today but any change. A death in the family is typically more traumatic if the family is legalistic. The change that death requires warns the legalist that there are risky decisions to be made. Legalistic families tend to deny the impact of such changes even though the family may be composed entirely of Christians.

Legalists exhibit more "wishful thinking" than nonlegalists. Such thinking tends to divert attention and energy away from effective problem solving and toward more egocentric thoughts of why God brought disaster on them. In another vein, legalistic Christians are least likely to vote in any election, unless to vote for a candidate associated with an approved cause such as prolife. They believe that the world is headed to hell in a handbasket anyway, and fighting the system will probably just prolong the agony.

"Holding on fast until the Lord comes" is a common refrain and solidly believed doctrine for legalists who have taken a retreatist posture when it comes to reaching the world for Jesus.

Coping Ability: Nonlegalistic Families

Nonlegalistic Christians exhibit a more realistic acceptance of stressors that impact the family. Though stress is unwelcome in all families, nonlegalistic families do a better job of accepting it and dealing with it well.

When stress surfaces, nonlegalistic Christian family members are more likely to be able to lean on one another and draw support. In legalistic families, the stress often drives family members away from each other rather than toward one another. In nonlegalistic families a problem is a challenge to grow in trusting God. In legalistic families a problem is punishment for sin, chastisement for a real or imagined affront to the Almighty, rather than an opportunity to learn to trust.

Nonlegalistic families are better able to demonstrate coping and problem solving to their children. Learning to be parents by first being children of parents applies to solving problems as it does to everything else. Childhood and adolescence are an apprenticeship for life, and if the master crafters (parents) are good at what they do, the youngsters will grow up showing a tendency to repeat what they saw in their parents.

Conclusion

We have looked at legalistic and nonlegalistic Christian families from the perspective of the work of the family. We have focused on communication patterns, emotional expressions, relationships, power structure, role differentiation, and coping abilities and the different ways families work them out.

If you are like me, you have seen something of yourself and your family in these pages. I am a recovering legalist, and everything negative I have discussed I was once a part of. I know how easy it is for any Christian to become ensnared in the seductive mesh of legalism. But God does not want any of us to put obstacles in the paths of our children, whether legalism or liberalism.

All parents question their own wisdom at times. When in doubt, their best possible course is to refer to the Bible and ask God for guidance, then learn to trust their sense of what is best for their families rather than to lean on legalistic, man-made formulas.

Finally, remember, love and legalism cannot co-exist.

5

Legalism and Family Violence

Reports of family violence are up. It is estimated that at least a million Christian women are victims of beatings by husbands each year in the United States. Some experts have concluded that between 25 and 30 percent of all American wives are battered by their husbands.

But violence is not limited to Christian women nor to women in general. A national study conducted as far back as 1980 found 60 percent of parents admitted to "hitting" their children. The circumstances of such hitting were not spelled out, but it is clear that much of this abuse occurs under the protective smokescreen of spanking.

A more recent survey of evangelical pastors, conducted by the National Association of Evangelicals, found that a great majority believed that church families were becoming more like unchurched families in all areas including child and spouse abuse. Whether in rural areas, cities, or suburbs, the increase in violence cuts across all socioeconomic, geographic, and religious boundaries.

This is not enjoyable to write nor to read, but the subject is important. Our concern is to be able to understand the nature of family violence and see its relationship to the degree of legalism practiced in a family. I firmly believe there is that strong connection between legalism and family violence.

I don't want to believe this is the case where Christians are involved, but available research and the experiences of many Christian counselors support this negative conclusion. Legalistic Christian families are prone to resort to violence to solve family problems, and the church is going to have to find ways to intervene to help these families. Christianity as a whole suffers when any of its members misconstrue it into un-Christian practice.

It is not difficult to see the connection, at least in potential, between a legalistic orientation and a willingness to use violence to solve a family problem. The following personal experience illustrates this point. I am concerned that the story may seem so outrageous it may be difficult to believe, but it is absolutely true, with no exaggeration whatever.

I happened to be in the hallway of a legalistic, separatist Christian university where I taught. It was almost a capital offense to talk in the halls during class times at this school. A door was open, and it was impossible not to hear the professor teaching adolescent psychology to a class of fifty to sixty juniors and seniors.

I do not know the context, but I do know that this professor was telling the students that while beating one's wife was generally not an acceptable thing to do, nevertheless if a wife refused to follow her husband's leadership and the husband believed that the *testimony* of the family would be hindered by her refusal, it was then "okay" to beat her until she submitted to his "spiritual leadership."

I stayed in the vicinity for several minutes, not really believing what I heard. But I had heard right. The professor even repeated it for effect and responded to questions from the students on that subject. Here was a Christian man with an earned doctorate teaching at one of the largest fundamentalist schools in America, telling these impressionable young people that it was acceptable, under certain circumstances, to use violence against another family member.

And note that the justification this college professor used to make his point was that the family might lose its *testimony,* a rationale completely consistent with all legalists' preoccupation with what other people think of them. (An amusing aside to this sad but true story is that Linda and I know this professor and his wife and if he ever actually did try to beat his wife, she would tear him apart.)

To distinguish between legalistic families and nonlegalistic families relative to family violence, we shall examine several important family functions that come to bear on it.

The Provider Function

To read the newspapers we might think otherwise, but most American families are still headed up by a male who serves as the primary provider of income and other resources for the family. Though this pattern continues to predominate, it is also true that approximately 57 percent of American women with school-age children are employed full-time outside the home. Mothers working has been a major change just in the last ten years and shows no sign of decreasing.

Many Christian husbands and fathers believe that they are personally and totally responsible for the actions of all family members and for making sure that all their needs are met. This "total provider" role can produce tremendous amounts of frustration if anything goes wrong, to say nothing of feelings of incompetence. Frustration can become violence in any situation or family, especially if the husband feels it is God's call on his life to meet 100 percent of the family's needs.

Nonlegalistic husbands and fathers tend to be better able to accept the shared-provider model: both parents sharing, although not equally perhaps, in family responsibilities including financial needs. A shared burden reduces not only financial stress but also lessens the likelihood that Dad will feel his manhood threatened when he is temporarily unemployed or facing some other challenge to his ability to provide for the family.

The unfortunate reality of America in the 1990s is that it is virtually impossible for a couple to buy a home on only one income. Legalistic Christian teaching often creates problems for a husband and father by insisting that he is less than he should be if his wife "has to" work. Depending on the extent of legalistic teachings in a church, many of its young married couples can really struggle with feelings of guilt over the wife's need to work.

Frustration leads to thoughts of violence, and thoughts become reality in too many Christian families. "Wives working" is another "rabbit trail" common to legalistic preaching and teaching and is usually taught or preached by a person wealthy enough to allow him to be pious on the subject.

Sex-Role Distinctions

Legalistic Christians don't like gray areas. The more clearcut an issue, the easier a person can be classified into one group or another, or the more quickly a person's church or Christian school background can be ascertained, the happier a legalist will be.

So a man is a man, and a woman is a woman, and never the twain should cross sex-role lines lest legalists become confused.

This need for classification and limitation can be expected eventually to became a source of frustration. At some point in a marriage, one or the other will be unable to perform the "assigned" duties because of illness or absence from the family. If Dad's job is making more demands on him so that his time for "chores" is reduced, he may become angry upon finding that Mom has tried to fill in for him. This was the situation with Peter and Valerie Climente. They were seeing me for marital counseling brought on by Peter's beating Valerie, the police being called, and counseling being mandated if he wanted to stay out of jail.

Peter, a typical legalistic Christian, did not want to be in counseling and felt that his "rights" as a husband had been violated when he was arrested. But he and his wife were in my office and Peter wore the typical "fix-me-if-you-can" expression I had seen so often in husbands from a strict legalistic family background.

We got started with some difficulty, but Peter began to volunteer his perspective that Valerie had begun to "invade his masculinity" by doing things around the house that he was having difficulty finding time for. Peter was talking about such ordinary things as fixing a leaky faucet in the bathroom and raking leaves in the yard. The kids were too young to help, and Valerie decided that she had time to do what her husband was too busy to do.

That's right. That's what Valerie did that brought a beating her way and the police into the Climente's living room.

But Peter had been taught by his legalistic pastor that man's work and women's work must not be mixed. Period. Blurring of the sexual dividing line was nothing less than sin, he had been taught, to say nothing of the wife's implicit commentary on his masculinity as well.

Frustration brought on by legalistic and unbiblical teachings (check Galatians 3:28, for example) had put this young husband in a corner, and he didn't know what to do but strike back.

Nonlegalistic families are much more accepting of a degree of flexibility and compromise when it comes to family roles and responsibilities. We are all strongly influenced by the family in which we were raised and we will tend to repeat the parenting and marital behaviors seen in our childhood unless something intervenes. Because nonlegalistic Christian couples are not continually reminded that it is their "duty" to maintain sexual polarization at home, when a situation arises that requires crossing sex-role lines, such as caring for a sick infant, the adjustment can be made without guilt feelings and embarrassment.

Decision Making

Who makes the decisions in your family? Who made the decisions when you were a child growing up? Are the answers the same? They usually are, and here again we see the issue of learning to be parents by first having been children.

Legalistic Christian families are characterized by authority figures making decisions alone. Every legalistic family is dominated by one or the other parent making decisions. Likewise, legalistic churches are frequently pastor led rather than board led. The reasons for this are usually stated in spiritual terms, such as "Father should be the final authority in all decisions involving the family." The problem surfaces when legalism teaches people that virtually all decisions are spiritual in some sense and so no one but Dad is *allowed* to take responsibility for family decisions.

Again, it is an easy step from decision domination to violence. Dad feels that he is overburdened with family responsibilities, possibly involving his job or threatened unemployment or illness in the family. He is making decisions on many fronts, and not every one turns out to be wise or heeded. He then experiences the typical frustration/aggression reaction and vents his anger and feelings of impotence by physically controlling or beating into submission other members of the family.

Does he know it is wrong to beat his family? Does he know it is not Christian to hurt others? Probably, but what if this husband and father had taken adolescent psychology from that Christian college professor I mentioned earlier?

I can almost hear comments such as "This wouldn't happen in a *really* Christian family." But it does. Fortunately, however, the majority of Christians are not legalistic and do not believe it is God's will that they beat up family members. True sharing of decision making reduces the opportunities for abuse by dispersing this burden as it should be dispersed equally between Mom and Dad.

Should a family be a totally democratic structure? No, it is not supposed to be democratic and would not survive if it tried to be. A Christian father does bear ultimate responsibility for spiritual decisions (Eph. 5:22–6:4) and the mother may find it necessary to agree when no compromises are possible. What church to attend, whether to send the children to Christian or public schools, how much to tithe and send to missionary activities are spiritual decisions, and though we would always hope that the parents would be so united in their sensitivity to the Holy Spirit that they would automatically agree, it does not quite happen that way in the real world.

However, legalistic Christianity puts the husband and father under more stress than God intended him to bear, and too often the result is family violence.

Nurturing/Strengthening

Nonlegalistic Christian families are led by parents who share in providing both nurture and strength. Such mutuality provides all members of the family with a sense of security founded on this double based family structure. It also provides the children with healthy, positive role models.

Police records clearly indicate that violence in the family usually means violence against the wife. Psychological research shows that many women in violent situations have come to expect the beatings as a normal part of being married, a lesson learned most often when they were children observing their own mothers being abused at the hands of their fathers.

Legalistic families are more likely than nonlegalistic to possess characteristics that lead to violence of some sort. In addition, research on church-based families also reveals a common attitude held by a large percentage of church leaders that a woman should put up with physical maltreatment as an aspect of biblical submission.

Consider this brief sample of the comments frequently heard by some Christian women who go to their pastors for help with being abused:

"Stay and work things out. God expects that."
"Try harder not to get him angry."
"He is a bum, but you married him."
"Christians can't divorce just because of abuse."
"Pray for him and hope for the best."
"Forgive and forget."

It doesn't take much effort to figure out what the upbringing of these pastors was like.

Nonlegalistic Christians generally have a different set of experiences, though. Wives in nonlegalistic Christian families typically do not choose to marry men who possess those characteristics leading to abuse. This is as much a subconscious process as planned, and stems from personality and discernment developed over many years of watching effective parents deal with each other. Further, Christian women in nonlegalistic churches are not going to be taught that the biblical thing to do is put up with the beatings "for the sake of the children" or for their "testimony."

Wives who are taught that it is God pleasing to be strong as well as compassionate and husbands who are taught that God smiles on a nurturing as well as strong man find each other and make good nonlegalistic families. But wives who are taught that women are not supposed to be strong and husbands who are taught that it is an exclusively feminine trait to be nurturing also find each other. It is this latter group who are likely to be in the counselor's office, the divorce court, or the police station at some point.

Conflict Resolution

Conflicts are opportunities awaiting wise decisions. Of the many tasks facing every family, resolving conflicts is always near the top in importance.

Legalistic Christian families learn to see problems and conflicts differently than do most other Christians. Problems and conflicts are perceived as persecution from the world for righteous living or as punishment from God for sinful living. Legalistic Christians have great difficulty understanding setbacks as nothing more than natural occurrences in anyone's life rather than as results of specific actions on their part.

Nonlegalistic Christians learn something very different about problems and conflicts. The reality that it does indeed "rain on the just and the unjust alike" is somehow easier to internalize for nonlegalists, putting them more at ease with themselves and their place in the world. Of course, there are times when specific consequences follow specific actions, good or bad, but nonlegalistic Christians seem to know better the truth proclaimed by Paul in Romans 5:3–4: "We glory in tribulations also; knowing that tribulation worketh patience; and patience, experience; and experience, hope."

Hope is the key element. The ability to see problems and conflicts as normal rather than abnormal, natural rather than supernatural, allows nonlegalistic Christians to negotiate, adjust, and compromise so that difficulties are resolved without the need to make major spiritual "decisions" at every turn, stressful decisions that tend to have defensive or authoritarian overtones. Christians who spiritualize the normal problems of life often become "aisle athletes," feeling the need to run to the altar in every church service to get special spiritual insights about what color Buick to buy.

Failure to solve problems and resolve conflicts leads to stress, which, we know, is always the prerequisite to family violence. When parents can share and demonstrate the ability to find solutions, the children feel safe and protected, the parents' self-concept goes up a notch, and God is pleased.

Personal and Spiritual Growth

We have looked at several stress-related factors already, but one is frequently and easily overlooked: the lack of personal and/or spiritual development in either or both marriage partners.

Research tells us that undereducated people are more likely to abuse their children, themselves, or their spouses. Isolated people, people who are lonely or feel rejected by others, and emotionally disturbed people are more likely to resort to violence under stress. And we know as well that *biblically undereducated* professing Christians are prone to family violence.

When legalistic Christians and nonlegalistic Christians are similar in income level, level of education, housing conditions, and other aspects of life, those in legalism tend to be at a lower level of biblical education and spiritual maturity. Legalism, for example, disenfranchises half the Christian population by declaring that the sole function of a woman is to be wife and mother, disregarding what may face a woman when she cannot have children, or when the children are grown, or when she is not able or willing to marry. Legalistic Christians following a male authority figure tend to accept the notion that education should be "reserved" for those who can most benefit from it. If the truth were known, the real reason so many legalists resist making secular or biblical education available to women is the fear that wives may "usurp" the authority that "rightly belongs" to men when the women learn of the true liberty that is available to them as Christians.

Generally, we find in legalism an entire chain of insufficient education, beginning at the highest levels of spiritual authority and trickling down in ever lessening amounts to those "beneath," including parents and, of course, children. I suspect that most legalists harbor true anti-intellectual biases, believing that too much education is really a dangerous thing. Such bias among legalistic leadership usually takes the form of suspicion about any kind of secular authority but in many churches and schools the bias extends even to church members who are trained professionals. Doctors, lawyers, business people, and the like are suspected of being "corrupted" by their education. A few recognized legalistic Christian colleges and universities are known for their inability to hire and retain qualified professors because of their leaders' suspicion and anti-intellectual bias.

The result of this trickle-down effect is that many Christian families exposed to legalistic teachings come to be suspicious of anyone with academic credentials, including Christian writers who raise difficult or confrontive questions as well as speakers who are not afraid to go into the public arena and debate the tougher issues.

The relationship of an anti-intellectual bias to family violence is complex, and reflects to the type of leadership in a particular church, the quality of the secular and biblical education of a married couple, and their own level of spiritual maturity. Ignorance is not bliss, it is ignorance, and personal ignorance once recognized causes feelings of inferiority that can lead to stress reactions and violence.

In legalistic families a wife had better not let her husband get the impression that she is better educated or more informed about *anything,* no matter what her intentions. A legalistic husband has been taught that he is not only the spiritual head of the home but the authority in all other areas as well. Many of the abuse referrals coming to me from family court involving Christian husbands originate from the point where that husband felt his "God-given authority" being challenged by a wife who simply knew more about something than he knew.

It is difficult to conclude a topic such as family violence, for something more always can be said. Legalistic teaching convolutes normal interactions by making a Christian husband feel he must keep up a family appearance at all costs, and if beating his wife is the only way he can attain this goal, then beat her he must.

Love does many things in the Bible, but one thing that love *never* does is hit.

Children

Children are both vulnerable and resilient.

How a certain child or teenager responds to a crisis depends on many elements including personality, the nature of the crisis, family teaching and support, and age. When it comes to matters of family violence, children raised in legalism tend to be more vulnerable than resilient. Parents convey to children either their power to bounce back from difficulty, or the opposite—that they cannot win their battles with the "world." That the negative aspect is more common in legalistic homes stems from the prevalent mind-set that sees trouble as judgment from God rather than as a time of testing that will lead to eventual victory.

So if a child or adolescent raised in legalism sees Dad beating Mom, the youngster's perception of that event will take on this perspective:

1. I have been taught that it is the wife's role to submit to her husband, and I guess if Dad as spiritual head feels violence is necessary to achieve a proper Christian home, then he is right in doing what I see him doing to Mom.

2. I have been taught that God uses physical correction in disciplining his children. I suppose, then, that car accident Dad had last month was to teach him something, and the same goes for my broken arm last year, though I still don't know what I did to deserve that. But if God sometimes "hits" us, then I guess it's okay if Dad sometimes hits Mom or one of us.

3. I have been taught that children are required to honor parents in all things, and even though I don't think the beatings are fair, the pastor tells us that Dad is always right when it comes to such things. I guess that is the way I will have to run my family someday, too.

Clearly, children in legalistic families and churches are taught that violence can be good at times, that fathers have not only a right but a duty to employ such harsh tactics, and when the kids grow up and have their own families, *their* children will have to submit to beatings just as they did. On several occasions I have heard a Christian father explaining his reasons for using what the law called abusive methods of child correction say, "I had to put up with beatings when I was a kid, so should my children be any different?"

These husbands and fathers are of *this* generation, not the last century. We delude ourselves if we think the problems identified in this chapter are rare. They may be uncommon in your group of Christians or mine, but they are predominant in other groups. This is legalism. The more legalism is practiced, the more violence occurs. We must not close our eyes to this.

6

Legalism and Child Discipline

H onestly, Dr. Miller, I just can't figure this kid out. He gets spanked at least once a day for disobedience, but he just keeps disobeying anyway. Why isn't he catching on? What can I do?"

"Listen, Doc, you and I both know I shouldn't have to be here talking to you. Sure, I might have spanked Billy a little too hard, and maybe the judge was right in telling me that the stick I used was too big for someone his size. But come on, Doc, I was just doing what the Bible tells me to do. Spare the rod and spoil the child. Right? That's all I was doing, Doc, just following what the Bible says to do when kids go wrong."

"Dr. Miller, I am a student in one of your child psychology classes and I am too embarrassed to tell you this in person. When you taught that lesson on what the Bible really says about child discipline, I could hardly keep from crying. You see, my dad believes that you are never too old to be spanked, as long as you are still living at home with your parents. I am trying to date a boy here at school whom my dad doesn't like.

Dr. Miller, I am almost twenty years old, and when I go home
at Christmas break and tell my parents that I am dating that
boy, he will try to spank me for disobedience!

"Dr. Miller, I would rather die than go through that again.
It is *so* humiliating at my age. But my dad says that is what
the Bible teaches and that is what he is going to do. I am so
depressed over this, I just don't know what I will do if he
tries to do that again. I have even considered suicide. Can
you help me?"

True stories, every one.

Concerns with discipline represent the number-one problem that brings Christian families into my counseling office.
Problems with disobedient children and adolescents. Questions about how much discipline is too much, and how little
is too little. Parents who are confused about Bible teachings
on the subject and concerned that the teaching they receive
in the church on this subject is often based only on Old Testament teachings. And concerns over why discipline that
seems to be biblical is not producing the hoped-for results and
what the parents may be doing wrong. Christian parents at
the point of questioning their own level of spiritual maturity
and biblical understanding because discipline hasn't worked.

All these issues and more are the currency of today's family counseling, and each is magnified and exaggerated by the
forces of legalistic teaching. The mice and the monsters are
sure to show up in the counseling office at some point.
Legalism compounds all family problems and reduces none,
and discipline is certainly no exception.

Principles of Child and Adolescent Behavior

Basic to all human behavior—and here we focus on child
behavior—are certain principles that operate in both legalistic and nonlegalistic families and result in both good and bad

behavior in children and teenagers. We want to be thoroughly consistent with biblical teachings on the subject.

Principle 1: All behavior is learned through interaction with the environment

Misbehavior and sin are inherent in all human beings. The Bible and natural history clearly and unavoidably attest to the universality of sin. Paul writing to the Galatian church reminded them and us that "The scripture hath concluded all under sin, that the promise by faith of Jesus Christ might be given to them that believe" (Gal. 3:22). Children need not be taught to sin, and it is not the environment that makes a child, adolescent, or adult a sinner. Rather it is humankind's original fall from grace through the disobedience of our original parents that brought sin into our lives. Human beings sin not because they are young or old, rich or poor, but because they are human beings and share a sin nature with all the rest of us.

But what children must learn is *how* to sin, the methods of their misbehavior. It is not the motivation to sin but the form that sin takes that is our concern here. And while it is not the environment that teaches a person to misbehave, it is the environment that teaches how to misbehave.

Both bad and good behavior are learned, and it falls to parents to assure that the good they teach outweighs the bad. The prime danger of legalism in this context is that once a family with children becomes "misbehavior reactive" instead of "good-behavior reactive," children or teens will quickly learn to obey and be well behaved not because they want to be good but because they are afraid of what will happen to them if they are bad. The result of this fear may appear to be the same as good-behavior reactive for a while: good behavior. But if the motivation for doing right is nothing more than fear of consequences for doing wrong, eventually the fun of misbehavior will smother higher morality, and bad behavior will surface again. Legalists typically have well-behaved children and poorly behaved teenagers and young adults. Once the youngsters in the family become old enough not to be so afraid of parents, their motivation to do right sometimes decreases and their motivation to do wrong increases. On the other hand, a nonlegalistic family may have less-well behaved children but much better behaved teenagers and young adults. One reason is that as children they were given more latitude for their behavior and were not taught to be afraid of parents. When independence arrives with adolescence and young adulthood, in the nonlegalistic family children have less need to overtly express their independence.

What can legalistic parents do to break this pattern? They can sit down together, just Mom and Dad, and seriously think about what they are trying to teach with their discipline. Is the goal simple obedience? Is it understanding and obedience? And who will make the final decision on how to discipline? Will it be Dad under the guidance of the Holy Spirit? Or will Dad and Mom still defer to an authority figure outside the family?

Once these questions are answered, the legalistic Christian family can start the healing process.

Principle 2: Children learn more by observing than by intentionally being taught

People learn best by watching and then by doing what they have observed. For most of human history the apprenticeship method of assigning a young person to help and watch a skilled older person was the most efficient way of teaching. When a young person wanted to become a carpenter, tinsmith, or physician, that person would hire on to work along with the master and eventually be able to work independently and even replace the older master at some point.

So it is with children. Moses set forth the basic pattern for children learning by watching their parents in Deuteronomy 6:6–7: "And these words, which I command thee this day, shall be in thine heart: and thou shalt teach them diligently unto thy children, and shalt talk of them when thou sittest in thine house and when thou walkest by the way, and when thou liest down, and when thou risest up."

"Do as I say and not as I do" is a common concept for parents trying to teach their children to do right without doing very much right themselves. Such hypocrisy inevitably leads to sending children to church alone, insisting that teenagers refrain from drinking while Dad keeps his stash of beer in the refrigerator, to say no to drugs while Mom and Dad are addicted to tobacco, and to refrain from premarital sex even though Mom and Dad have done a poor job of behaving themselves sexually.

Legalistic parents are clearly less likely to commit these more obvious sins, but they are more likely to preach the importance of loving all people while insisting that their Christian day school not admit blacks, or boldly proclaim the need to reach all people with the gospel while reserving special seats at the rear of the sanctuary for people who dress "inappropriately" for a church service. A legalistic parent, as do all parents, teaches more by behavior than words.

When counseling with families I often find very real and serious problems showing up in teens from Christian homes led by parents who seem to be all they should be on the outside but are critical, judgmental, and suspicious on the inside (typical of legalistic Christians). I have learned over the years that any family can look good but be terribly corrupt in secret. Legalism is often at the core of such problems because of its teaching the importance of maintaining outward appearances no matter what the inward spiritual condition. Legalism teaches that the measure of one's success as a Christian is measured by the opinions of others.

What can be done?

Once again, the cure begins with self-examination and a careful study of what the Bible *really* says on some of the more common child rearing principles of legalistic Christianity.

My experience has been that it is extremely difficult to get legalistic parents to look beyond the extrabiblical dictates of their church leaders or family experts to try to discover the principles and spirit of Christian human relationships in the Bible. To help them to use those principles in understanding and handling their own children can be even more difficult. But for them to do so is an essential part of their healing.

Principle 3: Behavior rewarded will occur more often than behavior preached

What else would we expect? Of course a reward will encourage a behavior to continue.

What is often overlooked when dealing with children, however, is that if a child or adolescent is being disciplined for misbehavior and the misbehavior continues anyway, there must be some kind of hidden reward continuing to reinforce the punished behavior. The reward that most readily comes to mind is the recognition from the parent the child gets by triggering the punishment. It is the only recognition, perhaps, and any recognition is better than none at all, even if it is not love.

"To obey is better than sacrifice" is the anthem of legalistic families and churches. Legalistic Christians stress conformity over independence, obedience over understanding, and loyalty over good judgment. This often leads to outwardly good behavior that masks inner turmoil. Many teenagers raised in legalistic families have revealed to me and others their secret methods of "beating the system"; by dressing right, having conservative haircuts, leaving gospel music tapes lying around for moms to discover, and hanging out with the right kind of young people as long as someone is watching, they cover their tracks or deflect attention from their devious behavior.

This duplicity leads legalistic Christian families to make either mice or monsters of their children. Monsters are less common than mice, because most families have been practicing legalistic Christianity since the children were very little, thereby almost completely smothering the children's tendencies toward independence. Once in a while we do hear of a young person from such a background being arrested for drug involvement or robbing a convenience store.

But the overwhelming majority of children from such families will become spiritual and psychological mice, afraid of the world and the people in it, convinced that things are moving in an irretrievably downward direction, and all they can do is dig in and hold on. Here the principle of rewarded behavior becoming dominant is seen at work: Children of legalists become well-behaved shells, because only conformity is rewarded; independence and free thinking are condemned as sinful, and new ideas judged to be unworthy. The price these children pay for becoming Christians who are moral, church attenders, doctrinally sound tithers, and who would never commit a sin knowingly is that they become less capable of original or creative thinking.

Principle 4: Behavior that is ignored or no longer rewarded will occur less often

Punishment is very effective in immediately stopping misbehavior. Punishment paired with teaching equals discipline, and discipline is strongly recommended in the Bible, as it is by secular experts. The challenge to parents is to know how much discipline is just enough but not too much, and to decide what kind is appropriate.

Nonlegalistic parents take things in stride. They have a better understanding and acceptance of children's behaviors or misbehaviors and are less threatened by them than are legalistic parents. They know children go through developmental stages that have characteristic behaviors. By not making too much of an incident—by not rewarding it with overattention or overly harsh punishment—they find that most such phases will pass and the children's sense of themselves remains undamaged.

Legalistic parents focus on sin, may be obsessed with it. So they believe, and their leaders tell them, there is no such thing as too much punishment. This can actually be self-defeating, for it is in direct opposition to the usually more effective method of generally ignoring day-to-day normal misbehavior.

Nonlegalistic parents tend more to talk things over with their children, helping the children to get perspective on their misbehavior in view of the basic Christian principles the parents wish to convey. And by gaining insight into the children's sensitivities they can better gauge the discipline for the least damaging, most effective type and amount.

Legalistic parents tend not to deal in thought and underlying principles, as we have seen, and so talking with their children takes on more the form of verbal punishment, harping on the sins that are better left de-emphasized.

Such legalistic emphasis on sin leaves little room in a soul for positive joy in the Lord. What a waste!

Principle 5: Behavior is determined by prior circumstances as well as controlled by consequences

Understanding the form any misbehavior takes and how that misbehavior can be controlled requires awareness of both antecedent and consequent events. Alert Christian parents will want to find out what happened immediately prior to the misbehavior that encouraged it and what happened or did not happen as a result of that misbehavior. Was it reinforced so that the child will want to do it again? What appropriate consequences will discourage it? Administering appropriate types and amounts of discipline with determination and resolve will control the greater portion of misbehavior in any family.

The same principles apply to encouraging good behavior. I was to emphasize that *encourage* is the key word of a major concept in Paul's instructions on Christian relationships. When good behavior occurs, effective parents reinforce it with reasonable rewards. Usually brief verbal praise or appreciation is sufficient, perhaps accompanied by a hug. Note that I do not advocate unreasonable or excessive praise or reward, particularly material reward, for that, too, can have unwanted results: superficial praise that becomes ineffective; praise that gives a child an inflated, unfair (to him or her) concept of self-importance; "buying" good behavior instead of encouraging self-discipline; spoiling a child who acts for reward instead of in love.

Remember, Christian parents have the perfect role model of a teacher who taught by emphasizing the positive: Jesus Christ.

Principle 6: Behavior is most efficiently controlled with a combination of reasonable punishment and reinforcement for improvement

In summary, then, this is known to work.

The criteria for successful child or adolescent discipline are (1) the effectiveness of the method and (2) whether or not the method is consistent with Bible teachings on the subject, for what works must be biblical. We know that moderation in method is important as is acknowledging improvement in behavior followed closely by positive reinforcement. For example, it may be effective to manipulate a child into obeying by lying about a nonexistent consequence. But lying violates a biblical principle and should be avoided.

Christian parents who discipline out of loving concern will at the same time be to their children models of Christian love. That, then, becomes the basis for the children's self-discipline—discipline's ultimate goal.

The Impact of Legalism on Family Discipline

Legalism is Christian extremism. Legalism is extreme in its teachings on life, church polity, family relationships, and spiritual matters. Legalism promotes an extreme emphasis on harsh physical methods of child and adolescent discipline, with harmful side effects. True, nonlegalistic parents may be abusive in their child discipline, too, and I know some who are. But the likelihood is greater when the teaching on the family comes from legalistic sources.

Extensive reliance on punishment
sets up escape/avoidance behaviors
in children and adolescents
that are often more harmful
than the behavior being punished

What is good behavior worth?

Future psychological damage? Being arrested for child abuse? Losing a marriage? Lifelong guilt?

The risk of all these negatives is greater when harsh and unreasonable discipline techniques are employed. Children and teens can be frightened into behaving themselves. The fear of pain is a basic human motivator known to the torturers of the Inquisition as well as to middle-eastern kidnappers.

Pain works!

In a family situation a child can become more afraid of the pain of punishment than the guilt of wrongdoing.

Some children will consider running away, even if it involves risk to themselves rather than face the sure certainty of pain inflicted by an angry parent. Instead of encouraging a child or teen to stay out of trouble, harsh methods teach avoidance and escape techniques that may last a lifetime. Legalistic Christian parents are likely to have been taught that spanking is the only way to discipline children biblically, and that the harder they are spanked the more likely the children will determine never to do the bad behavior again.

But wishing won't make it so. Harsh physical methods are ineffective when compared with less painful physical methods or such tactics as isolation and timeout. God always reserves physical methods for the time when nothing else has worked. Spanking is biblical, yes, but it is supposed to be used sparingly and reasonably and only when all else has failed.

Extensive punishment establishes emotional reactions that may be harmful

Anxiety is the common reaction seen in children whose parents rely heavily on physical methods to correct behavior. A child or teen becomes anxious over the coming pain but also experiences anxiety over the possibility of receiving the pain again for a future offense. For parents who are taught that God only smiles on physical punishment, there is a real and present danger of child abuse as well as emotional hurt for both parent and child.

Christian counselors can attest to the damage done by harsh physical methods. Hard feelings toward both parents are common, even though the father usually is the punisher. Dad receives the brunt of negative emotions because of being the pain provider. Mom receives negative feelings because, to a child's mind, she allows Dad to administer the pain. Maybe she even asks Dad to do it. Even if some childish irrationality prompts these memories and emotions, they often remain powerful for many years.

Extensive punishment may produce guilt feelings in parents

Legalistic Christian parents are more likely to do as they have been taught and so are more at risk for all negative reactions, including personal feelings of guilt. Experiences of families whom I have counseled are never pretty, including their guilt.

Parents may feel guilty if they discipline as harshly as they have been taught by a church authority figure, or they may feel guilty if they do not discipline as they have been taught. With no shortage of authority figures in legalistic churches and schools just waiting for an opportunity to impose their extra-biblical ideas on child rearing on the unsuspecting, parents' guilt burdens are common.

Guilty if they do, guilty if they don't. Legalism extracts a high price from Christian parents in exchange for the temporary security that comes from simply doing what they are told.

Punishment may produce compliance, but the behavior will likely reappear

Even legalistic parents would not rely exclusively on heavy-handed punishment to stop an unwanted behavior, but they are prone to use excessive punishment to keep their youngsters under control. Punishment is effective in stopping a bad behavior, but once the punisher is away from the child or teen, the motivation to misbehave will return and a repetition will occur.

This happens for two reasons. First, punishment does not eliminate the reason for the bad behavior, so even though a spanking took place yesterday, today is another story. Second, if punishment is going to produce the desired effects, it must be administered each time the misbehavior occurs, an obvious impossibility. The scenario of misbehavior, punishment, and then misbehavior again dogs the path of every legalistic parent.

Harsh methods do not eliminate the motivation for wrongdoing; they teach that there is a price to pay if caught, but only if caught.

Punishment loses effectiveness with frequent and prolonged use, leading to more severe methods

Youngsters do not become used to having pain inflicted on them. Rather, they learn to cope with the pain and embarrassment and divert some of that negative energy into strong feelings against the punisher. Misbehavior will only stop permanently when the youngster is disciplined in such a way that punishment gradually decreases while teaching increases. I agree with many experts who feel that as a child grows, he or she should need less and less correction each year simply because they are "catching on" to the family rules and regulations.

Legalistic Christian parents, though, are likely to have become locked into one "right" way of dealing with child or teen misbehavior and will be reluctant to change. The fact that a parent may be getting dangerously close to child abuse problems may cause a decrease in the use of harsh methods; but the parent, usually the father, may just "get his back up" and blunder ahead into conflict with the authorities. Remember, legalistic families are known to be significantly more at risk for child abuse prosecutions than secular families or other Christians.

If physical methods are overused, a parent may become a model of aggression for the child

Our first child, Laurie, was about three years old and in the process of becoming toilet trained. One day Linda observed Laurie holding her kitten over the toilet while firmly commanding, "Go!"

We took care to let her know that the process is different for kittens, but the lesson that stayed with us was how strongly children are influenced by what parents do to and for them. No, we had never held Laurie over the toilet as she did with her kitten, but that simply illustrates the problem. Children easily translate our behavior into something they can deal with.

Parents who employ harsh methods may be completely motivated by love and a desire for God's best for the children. But good intentions are not always correctly translated by children. We teach by our behavior, not our intentions. A child being spanked only notices the pain and atmosphere of violence, nothing else. Perhaps later, as the pain subsides, a child may correctly reflect on the meaning of what happened. But parents had better not assume that the lesson is correctly learned. We know that "bullies" frequently have aggressive, violence prone fathers who firmly believe in physical methods. If a parent wants to keep violence in check for a youngster, that parent needs to be careful about teaching by example.

The punishing parent loses effectiveness and power

Any parent's value as a positive force in the life of a child will decrease in exact proportion to the amount of pain the child feels at the hands of a parent. A child may know the family dentist as a great guy who lives next door and likes to play catch. But if that neighbor dentist has hurt that child during treatment, there will be no more playing ball. The parent who hurts the child will see his or her power and influence weaken as the child or teen learns to avoid the source of the pain.

Even if in adulthood children come to understand that their parents loved them in spite of the fact that they hurt them, they continue to have their negative feelings toward the punishing parent. It is sad to listen to clients sitting in my office tell how they still cannot stir up positive feelings toward their strict and punitive fathers who often beat them when they were children.

When all is said and done, we want our children to grow up knowing that we love them and want the best for them. Again the question before us is what is the right type and amount of discipline. No one can speak for your family but those who belong to it, but it is clear to me from searching the Bible that the relative silence on this issue in the New Testament and the general rather than specific teachings in the Old Testament reveal that many Christian parents today are out of proportion when it comes to child discipline. Many have made an idol of the "rod" and believe that this physical act is the cornerstone of good Christian parenting. This is particularly sad, because unconditional love like we receive from God is the real cornerstone of the family, and so much more fun to share.

Have you seen yourself in these comments?

Do you want to know how to find out if you are being excessive or inappropriate in your discipline? There is a way. Put down your child-expert books and pick up your Bible. Read for yourself what God does and does not say about disciplining children. Notice that physical methods are always reserved as a last resort when God is doing the discipline. Notice that Jesus has nothing at all to say on child discipline but everything to say on compassion and love, and that virtually all of the passages used to teach the importance of spanking are found in one book of the Old Testament (Prov. 13:24; 19:18; 22:15; 23:13; 29:15).

Then pray for guidance from the Holy Spirit, and determine to pray alone each time you feel that a spanking might be in order. These practices will help you find a biblical and humane perspective on discipline.

7

The Child Acquires an Identity

A high percentage of the children of legalistic Christian parents reject legalism in their own lives. In spite of the obvious difficulties such a departure must involve, breaking away from legalism seems to be increasing in the younger generation of Christians. This change is not limited to children. The most legalistic Christian colleges and universities saw their enrollments halved in the decade of the eighties. Legalistic churches are losing ground to less negative and exclusive churches. Legalistic pastors, too, find their preaching opportunities shrinking.

But even under the most optimistic predictions, it will be many years before the negative effects of legalism will be significantly diminished.

Yes, the days when an authoritarian pastor could dictate college choice for the young people in the church are gone. The decision is a family decision, and often an individual decision made by the young person. And of course it has been the college experience that has historically allowed dogma and preference to be taught with holy forcefulness. However, there will long be a need for counselors and others to prepare spiritual and psychological first aid for the refugees from this extreme form of Christianity.

In large part the journey from babyhood to adulthood involves developing an identity. A newborn is unaware of much beside him or herself, but to friends and relatives the baby's identity is the parents': "Jean and Carl's baby." Before long, however, the baby becomes increasingly aware of the parents, and then of him or herself in relation to those parents. Over the years the child assimilates what the parents are as persons and, subconsciously usually, becomes much like the parents—identifies with the parents.

At the same time, the child works to develop his or her identity: decisions about who and what he is, what are his preferences and goals, his tastes and choices, what about his parents he accepts and rejects, becoming an independent person in his own right.

Children raised in Christian homes also either assume for themselves or reject their parents' values and behaviors. God has no grandchildren, and every person must make his or her decision about Christ. Nevertheless, that decision cannot help but be influenced by the person's identity with or desire to be like his Christian parents.

Two important aspects of identification may help in understanding how and why a legalistic orientation is or is not passed from one generation to another. The process of identification allows children to model their parents' good qualities. It is also the process of identification that convinces many to remain behind the barricades of legalism.

Our attention is on two very important elements that lead children to identify with parents: love and power, which equally apply to the understanding of Christian legalism.

The Importance of Love to Identification

A family without love is not a family, it is a prison.

A family without love cannot function as a family in even the slightest sense. Love is expressed or unexpressed in countless ways, but we will examine only those that surface most often in counseling Christian families struggling with the bonds of legalism. Those who suffer at the hands of legalism are missing some or all of the following good parental qualities.

Warmth and nurture are the most important things parents convey to children

Parents must see themselves more as reinforcers than as punishers or disciplinarians. To facilitate a child's wanting to be like them parents must allow their warmth and nurturing tendencies to rise to the top. Ordinarily this is not a problem. Doing things with the children, asking about their day, listening to their concerns, comforting their pains are crucial but to be expected. And each teaches love.

The Bible reminds us that nothing can separate us from the love of God. Parents must be careful to love their children unconditionally and to let them know that they are loved unconditionally. Of course, God and parents care about even the smallest of behaviors, but not to the extent of withdrawing love when a failure occurs. Parents love their children no less when they are bad. They may not *like* children when they throw tantrums or announce that they have an unexpected three-day vacation from school for making disgusting noises during civics class.

Good parents who effectively transfer Christian values to their children do so because they are pleasant company to the children, affectionate, filled with joy and humor, and able to take teasing. Good parents are not threatened personally by anything a child or teenager does, are secure in their own sense of worth, and do not feel they are failures because junior has a bad day at school.

Legalists can be good, loving parents, too, and often are, but the problems often surface when the first child enters adolescence and gets into some kind of trouble. And the problems are usually intensified because legalists have an altogether different standard of what constitutes getting into trouble from most other Christians and the general population.

What often happens is that a once well-behaved child has begun to feel the stirrings of independence and has begun to test the limits of school or home. I mentioned earlier that legalists tend to have well-behaved children and difficult teenagers, and once that independence surfaces and resembles rebellion, legalistic parents tend to overreact.

Of course, they don't have to overreact, and I know many parents who are confirmed legalists who do not overreact, but most will. Legalistic Christian parents turn their anger over the teen's misbehavior onto themselves and ask the question common to *all* legalistic Christian parents, "What did we do wrong?"

This need to blame, which is not universal but is very common in legalistic families, typically then leads to blaming the teen for "embarrassing the family and the Lord," as if Jesus were personally responsible for what the youngster did that got him into trouble.

For those legalistic parents who can control their tendency to be critical and judgmental of themselves and their children—who can be warm and nurturing—the process of identification can proceed, and the children will stand a good chance of growing up to espouse the same beliefs and values as they saw in their parents. But the evidence of more and more grown children of legalistic parents leaving this brand of Christianity is that too many parents still are coldly legalistic so that their children do not want to identify with them.

Parents are physically present to interact with their children

Identification is facilitated when parents are present in the home. The lower divorce rate for Christian marriages shows that those parents are more likely to be home when the kids need them. But the question is, What kind of parent-to-child or parent-to-teen interaction takes place? The mere fact that Dad is at home every evening will only encourage identification to take place if Dad is a person the kids would want to grow up to be like. If Dad is a gargoyle when he is at home, it is reasonable that the kids will not want to be around him nor want to be like him, and identification will not take place as completely.

In this connection is the observation that children of legalistic pastors, missionaries, and other full-time Christian workers rarely see their own children "called" into the ministry as they have been. Of course, this may simply be that God has in fact not called these young people into his service. But it could also be that the brand of Christianity practiced at home was so unpleasantly legalistic that God's call on some young people has fallen on criticism-hardened ears.

The parents' lifestyle is clear and consistent

For legalistic parents a problem is that children are hard to deceive, intentionally or otherwise. In legalistic families we find more unhappiness, suspicion, and questioning of motives than we see in nonlegalistic families. These negatives have chased more than a few young people away from the good Christian values held by parents, values that have become masked in suspicion, distrust, and pessimism. The comments I hear in my counseling office from grown children of legalistic parents reflect disillusionment with their parent's public "brand" of pious Christianity and their negative, bigoted, suspicious Christian life at home. Conversely, though rarely, Christian parents may practice legalism at work and in public but not take it home with them.

"If that's what it means to be a Christian," the children say, "I want no part of it."

Obviously, then, children will more easily identify with their parents' brand of Christianity when they love and respect their parents and there is no confusion as to what those parents' values are, legalistic or nonlegalistic.

The parents' expectations of children and teens are consistent and reasonable

Kids cope.

Children and teens can adjust and cope under all but the most extreme of circumstances, but they cannot adjust and cope when expectations by parents are inconsistent or unreasonable.

Why would Christian parents be unreasonable or inconsistent? One reason is that some legalistic Christian parents believe in separation and isolation from the world so intensely that it affects virtually every aspect of personal and family life. This leads to suspicion about the motives not only of non-Christians but even of Christians who do not belong to their "camp." Though this may sound extreme, my experience is that *all* forms of legalism are extreme. Bigotry develops naturally as a result of the isolation a family commonly practices and "others" become more and more remote from a family's personal experiences.

The second reason is that many legalists lead double lives—legalistic and pious when at church or with religious leaders, but softer and more compassionate at home. This religious "schizophrenia" of being one person there and another here is sensed by children and causes them to be uncertain of their parents' true beliefs. Worse, it means the parents themselves are unsure of their beliefs, and being unsure of themselves cannot clearly differentiate their expectations of their own children. Hence their inconsistencies. Yet, being legalists, they tend to overreact in their positions. No wonder the kids are confused and frightened.

During the first fourteen years of our family Linda and I belonged to the second type of legalists, able to accept legalism at church but keeping the home environment relatively free from its negatives. This was possible only because neither Linda nor I earned our living from ministry. She was a registered nurse and I was then a public school teacher.

But when the Lord called us into full-time service everything changed. Within a few months we went from secular employment to working and living in a legalistic Christian university environment. Linda was in charge of the obstetrical unit at the campus hospital, and I taught undergraduate psychology courses. We were quickly integrated into this Christian community. Families took meals together in one large dining hall. We were shoulder to shoulder with others in this environment for three meals a day, seven days a week. Our children attended school on campus, and except for an occasional trip to the grocery store or shopping mall, we could have spent twenty-four hours a day every day within the boundaries of this Christian community.

There were many good aspects to this arrangement. The children were safe as they never had been before. Our entire family lived *only* with other Christians and *only* with Christians living this particular form of legalism. But it was no longer possible to keep legalism in the church and out of the home. Everyone knows what others are doing in this kind of environment. Children talk to and about one another, parents ask questions; there are virtually no secrets and very little personal privacy. Though it took several years for us to realize what was going on, we were in fact becoming indoctrinated into extreme legalism, and at the time it felt pretty good.

Our three children experienced adjustment difficulties right from the start, though Linda and I did not notice what was really happening. Unable to articulate their feelings very well, the extremism and isolation were frightening the children and threatening their sense of security. This was strange to comprehend years later, because we thought the kids would have felt more secure in this very controlled environment. What was really taking place was that they saw their parents being replaced by the institution, and we were not aware of this. We lived six years in this environment. The negative impact remains powerful and still surfaces at times.

Our three children, now grown, are still confused about what was happening to their parents during those years, and I suspect that this will not be cleared up for some time. What Linda and I are both very sure about now is that legalism made it just about impossible for us to be the same consistent and loving Christian parents we always had been. This profound awareness is a major reason for the existence of this book: part psychological and spiritual healing for us, but an equal part desire that others in legalism will see something of themselves and their situation and be able to break free before serious family damage occurs.

The parents accept their roles as models for their children

It is important that parents know they are examples for the kids. Both good and bad parents are role models for their children. All parents—Christian or not, legalistic or not, aware of it or not—tell their children with equal force by word and action the way to live. The major influence on parents is the model of their own parents.

I have seen that many Christian parents raising children in a legalistic environment fail to show evidence of enjoying their life as Christians. They unconsciously tell their children by their sour attitude, gloomy pessimism, and defeatist mind-set that they are just "pilgrims," sort of treading water while trying to keep their heads out of the sewage of the world until Jesus comes to rescue them.

A sad and defeated way to live, this legalism. Its families become devoid of spontaneous happiness, everyone judging everyone, fearing God more than loving him, and never sure that they are truly loved, while authoritarian leaders live above the trials of normal life because of their "position."

Christian parents who love their children as God loves them are not afraid to take their children to an amusement park to have fun, even though this legalist or that might criticize them for being too "worldly." Such Christian parents model their "child-of-the-King" position in this world in contrast to the "worm-of-the-earth" position so often modeled by legalistic Christian parents. (A thirteen-year-old boy said to his legalistic father at a state fair one day, "Dad, why are you looking around? Are we doing something wrong?")

Christian parents who model happy, unafraid, accepting love for their children are models of the unconditional, accepting, forgiving love that we see in the life of Christ.

The Power of Power in Identification

Some people are turned off when power is mentioned in conjunction with Christian living, apparently believing that all power is bad. But I wonder if we are being fair if we deny the role of power in childrearing. Surely power can be used for good as well as evil. Think of the power of God in creation. Parents are every child's first god, after all, and Christian parents will want to convey a sense of God's omnipotence through their own expression of compassionate power in the family.

Power is also necessary for guidance, and without the ability to assert power with children and teens, the ability to protect and defend is diminished. One of the clearest uses of power was shown to me by a friend who was an elementary school principal. She was showing me around her school one morning when a child turned the corner at breakneck speed and accelerated down the hallway.

"Stop!" was the immediate command from this principal, followed by a seemingly instantaneous screeching halt.

"How in the world did you train these kids to obey you so quickly?" I asked.

"We work on this quite a bit in this neighborhood," she told me. "There are so many ways for children to be injured that I have to develop my power to get an immediate response from them for their own safety."

No muscle was used in this training, just calm encouragement backed up by consistent rewards and consequences. Surely any parents would want at least this minimum level of power in the family as well.

Here are some of the "make-a-difference" factors in the development of power in the family that leads to children identifying with their parents.

Parents are needs providers

Identification is encouraged when parents accept their position and responsibilities related to meeting the needs of the family. Small children have no trouble learning this important fact through daily interactions with their general environment and their own family. While still very young they learn that their survival depends on what their parents provide for them. Only at a later stage and only in some families do we see children and teens acting as if their parents need them more than they need their parents.

Cults always work to convince potential members that the leadership will meet their basic needs and they should not worry about such mundane things. While not strictly cultic, some legalistic institutions, and by that I mean larger churches, colleges and universities, and mission boards subtly convey that it is the institution that meets the needs of the family and not the parents.

Another personal experience illustrates this. At the legalistic Christian university where Linda and I worked, faculty and staff, as I have mentioned, were expected to take all their meals on campus in a common dining facility. A family could choose to eat at home, but meals were provided as a part of the financial package that made up the family salary. It was only years later, after we had left this university, that we realized our children had thought they were being provided for not by their parents but by the university.

Who was feeding our children? The institution. Who was providing "free" schooling for the kids? The institution. Who was controlling which house we lived in? The institution. And with whom were the children expected to identify? You guessed it. The institution!

I personally know of no cases where children "reported" misbehavior by their parents in this institution, but I would be very surprised if such has not happened at least a few times. I know of several families who experienced turmoil because Mom or Dad expressed opinions contrary to what was being taught at school; in fact, faculty and staff at this school constantly were reminded to be consistent at home. This meant, of course, that what was said at home should square with the official "line" coming out of the institution.

Does legalism make parents weak? Of course, it does. And does legalism subvert the identification process? Absolutely!

Parents use power as they deal with the environment

People are never attracted to weakness. This applies as well to family members as to anyone. Christian parents who behave as though they really believe what they proclaim in church will reflect a sense of confidence in self and in the God who protects. Both legalistic and nonlegalistic parents can do a good job of teaching by their example that both the world and the God who made it have power over people.

However, legalistic parents are more likely to adopt the attitude I saw in Barry, the young man I told about in a previous chapter who worked with me on the paint crew that summer: "If you deal with the world, you've got to expect to get beat up."

Like Barry, legalistic Christian parents tend to be so frightened of the world's power that they cannot help but reflect that fear to their growing children, thereby helping to convince them that God may not be able to help them overcome the world as he has promised.

A good friend with children roughly the same ages as ours was asked by his sixteen-year-old son if he could take a job he had been offered as a lifeguard at the local community swimming pool. Several lifeguards were to be hired, and this teen was a certified Red Cross swimming instructor who would qualify. He really wanted this job.

His father asked me what I thought he should do and said that he felt uncomfortable with the idea and needed to pray about it. I didn't ask him what his concern was with what seemed to me to be a pretty good job opportunity for a sixteen-year-old.

My friend refused permission to his son because, to use his terms, "There is just too much skin exposed on girls today with bathing suits, and I wouldn't want you to be tempted like that day after day."

Of course his son was very disappointed, but in good legalistic fashion did not dare to question his father's logic, at least not outwardly.

I couldn't help reflecting on the lesson this refusal probably taught the son: "You can't accept the job, because I can't trust you to be able to resist temptation, and I don't really believe God will protect you and keep you strong, either." What a lesson!

Where was the power? This father told his son that not only did the son have insufficient God-given power to resist temptation, but there was not even a suggestion that maybe God would do for this young man what his dad didn't believe he could do for himself.

Back to the barricades. Back to isolation. Back to feeling like a weak Christian with a weak God. Back to feeling like a moral failure just waiting to happen.

Parents discipline powerfully

Powerful discipline is not necessarily physical punishment. As a matter of fact, physical punishment is usually the least effective form of child control available. What really matters is the perception of the child related to the discipline being experienced. Parents, legalistic and non-legalistic, need to be concerned with whether or not the child or teen senses power in the disciplining parent and whether or not the behavior was worth it.

The important question is why the child or teen is being disciplined. Does the misbehavior stem from unreasonable expectations by parents? Is a learning disability or hyper-activity involved? Was the behavior careless or malicious? Legalistic Christian parents are much more likely to attach undue significance to relatively minor misbehavior. A phone call from school equals family disgrace and the end of all happiness. A sharp word spoken back to a parent on impulse reveals a total lack of spiritual maturity. Forgotten homework reveals hidden rebellion. Everything and anything may equate with sin to legalistic parents, leading to serious doubts about the spiritual condition of any young person who misbehaves. Resorting to these doubts becomes a powerful tool of discipline, at least in those parents' way of thinking.

My experience is that the more legalistic a person, the greater the need to label everything, and the labels become power instruments. The child or teenager is now a Christian (label) and so we would not expect that kind of behavior (label) from a saved kid. No Christian young person would talk back to his mother, would he?

Well, of course he would; he's human, isn't he? He takes after his mom and dad doesn't he? Didn't God say that all have sinned and come short of the glory of God? Well, talking back is *this* youngster's shortcoming right now.

Legalistic Christian parents also tend to evaluate their own performance as parents by the behavior of their children. To the extent that any Christian parent wants to accept responsibility for the unacceptable behavior of a child or teen, that parent will be perceived as a weak link in the family structure. Loving perhaps, but also weak. However, real strength and power in parents is revealed when mom and dad refuse to blame themselves for what another human being has done, even if that human being is one of their own children.

Christian parents exhibit power to their children and encourage imitation by being God-like in discipline. Christian parents, legalistic or not, trust God to direct them as disciplinarians for the family. The power of the Holy Spirit to lead and direct is acknowledged and accepted in families with powerful parents.

Love and Power of Christ

What leads us to want to be like Jesus is his love for us and his power over all the world. We cannot be that perfect, of course, but to the extent possible we want to demonstrate the love and power of God in us.

Parents who love their children love them enough to say both yes and no, yes to trusting God to protect even in difficult places like public swimming pools with all that exposed skin, and no when the time is right and the temptation too strong. Both legalistic and nonlegalistic parents are capable of demonstrating the love and power to their children that reflect the love and power of God.

What parents are and teach children in those early years will last a lifetime and beyond. However, the fact that some parents may misunderstand the loving nature of God does not change God's nature. But if they fail to carefully demonstrate unconditional love and compassionate discipline to their children, they come dangerously close to cheating their children out of a model of God's love and compassion and of such a God with whom the children will wish to identify. Any other model of God is unbiblical.

Yet, when parents and children prayerfully search Scripture for that model to follow, God in his love reveals it to them, and they experience a change that lasts a lifetime.

8

Legalism and Person-to-Person Interaction

My goal is to facilitate an understanding of Christian legalism. My desire is that Christians will, as my family has, symbolically join "Legalists Anonymous" and put artificial and ungodly separations and limitations behind them.

Their interpersonal behaviors and relationships reveal as much about Christian legalists and their makings as anything. My premise is that they are substantially different in many ways from nonlegalistic Christians, particularly in their perceptions of and subsequent interactions with other Christians and with people in general.

Legalists' Erroneous Bases for Perceiving Others

Legalists more than others have a need to form impressions of people before they decide if and how they will

127

interact with them. But they base their perceptions on very shaky ground to begin with—on errors in their premises for knowing and judging people. In this chapter we will examine those errors most common to legalists.

If you are a recovering legalist as I am, I believe you, too, will see something of yourself in these words. If you are not personally involved in this modern perversion of traditional Christianity, you will surely recognize those who are. As each of us moves toward greater freedom under God, our understanding of legalism's true colors makes the unconditional love of God all the more attractive.

Error 1: Inadequate Information

Legalists fear and despise ambiguity.

Ambiguity puts the fear of personal responsibility for deciding whether to develop a relationship with a new acquaintance squarely in their faces and demands that it be paid immediate attention. The fear of such decision making leads to immediate labeling, pigeonholing, categorizing—any means to get a handle on people and their situations.

"I must know where you stand," proclaims the legalist. "Tell me what Christian college you attended. Tell me the name of your church and what denominational affiliations are involved. Tell me where your pastor went to seminary.

"Tell me, please, does your pastor cooperate with Billy Graham? Jerry Falwell? James Dobson?

"Do you pray toward Greenville? Nashville? Dallas? Lynchburg?

"Please give me the answers. Can't you tell how much pain I am in knowing only that you are a Christian? I want to feel better when I am with you."

Is this unrealistic? Not if you have been around legalists very much.

Legalists get erroneous impressions of people based on inadequate information, because they ask the wrong questions and because once they make an error they are reluctant to admit to it and make the needed corrections.

Most people who realize they were wrong about someone probably say to themselves, "Oh well, I guess I was all wrong about Charlie," make whatever apologies or adjustments are needed, and move on.

But not legalistic Christians who are wrong. These folks are not disposed to admitting errors in judgment or perception, because of the authoritarian elements that predominate their personalities. Admitting an error equals a reduction in their "authority." Invariably, when an error is revealed that cannot be avoided, the tactic will be to rationalize the mistake, leading to statements such as, "I am sorry for assuming that you are not a Christian. I guess it was the leather jacket and motorcycle boots that fooled me."

Do you see what happened?

The legalist's reliance on externals proved to be wrong, but rather than simply apologize for the error, the legalist attempts to pass the buck and rationalize that it was another external—this person's clothing—that was responsible for the mistake instead of the legalist's mind-set. Or hair length. Or associations. Or church denominational affiliation.

You have probably noticed how so many followers of exposed and "defrocked" television evangelists simply would not accept that their spiritual leader could have done such an awful thing as visit a prostitute or buy gold-plated bathroom fixtures with tithes and offerings. There is in the orientation of legalists a belief that to admit sin is to admit weakness, and if there is anything important to legalists it is that they be perceived as powerful. Of course, not all followers of TV preachers are legalistic, and most television preachers are upright and godly people, but the pattern fits in many cases.

While making broad, "global" judgments and decisions based on inadequate or misperceived information is a common interpersonal error common among legalistic Christians, there is a cure, but it is a bitter pill for most to try to swallow. It is that friends and relatives need to constantly remind the legalists of past errors in making such judgments and that they seem to be heading down that same path again. The effectiveness of this is often sabotaged, though, because legalistic Christians are surrounded by other legalistic Christians who support rather than confront these errors in judgment.

Ultimately, the Bible is the answer to the errors of the legalist. The unconditional love of God shown to people regardless of their wealth or poverty, possession, or personal appearance is what matters. That Jesus was truly impartial is our example on how to break free of the excesses of Christian legalism.

Error 2: Implicit Personality Theory

It is a common human tendency to assume that similarity in background, upbringing, belief system, and church experiences make for familiar bedfellows. Legalistic Christians do not merely make decisions about a person's honesty, competence, and judgment but also about whether that person is going to wind up in heaven or hell. The "outer man" is the best indicator of the "inner man" for the legalistic mind.

What effect does this have on everyday life? If a Christian believes that a person's spiritual condition can be accurately perceived through examination of his or her appearance and companions, the next logical step is to change those factors. Legalists do not believe that clothing style or abstinence from tobacco gets a person into heaven. But they do believe that a person on his or her way to heaven will dress and act "like a Christian." No "real Christian" would attend the movies or drink wine at meals; therefore, a person who does these things must not be a "real" Christian.

And so the logic goes.

Thus we see the dividing asunder of all people into two groups, us and them, and legalists can tell who is "them" by the way they look or act or with whom they associate. The legalists' assumptions about what motivates people allows them to categorize every person.

This implicit personality theory and set of assumptions about people leads legalistic Christians to formulate extremely detailed dress and clothing "codes" for students in Christian schools, colleges, and universities. Hair above the ear and off the collar is what any "Christian" young man would want to have, isn't it? Certainly no "respectable" Christian young lady would be seen in public without pantyhose, would she? No Christian worth anything would eat in a restaurant that served liquor, would he?

The legalists' or their leaders' personal tastes as to proper appearances reveal to them, they believe, the essence of other people's personalities or spiritual conditions.

Error 3: Stereotyping

A stereotype is a broad, general belief that a person is unvaryingly similar to a group, another person, or narrow pattern of thinking or acting. Stereotyping holds that all Catholics (or Jews, Presbyterians, Mennonites, or whatever faith) are similar in some identifiable way to everyone else who is Catholic, simply because they are Catholics. Conformists are always stereotypical thinkers, and the ranks of legalists are filled with conformists who stereotype other people.

The need to stereotype is based on the need to know (that hated ambiguity mentioned earlier). Stereotyping is bigotry in any form, and no less so when it is proclaimed by a Christian. Labels and categories are the currency of legalism and are based on the belief that "all" people who are (fill in your own blank here) are like each other. It is inconceivable to think of Jesus or Paul lumping all people together based on their skin color, religious affiliation, or country of origin, yet this is common for legalists to do.

A further comment on the racial component in legalism might be in order. It is my personal belief that all legalists are racist in some degree. The very nature of legalistic beliefs is exclusionary, egocentric, and culturally arrogant. Whether the legalism is found among Moslems, Mormons, Jehovah's Witnesses, or fundamentalist Christians, the basic belief structure is inevitably based on the assumed superiority of one's own race over all others.

One of the hardest lessons I had to learn as a new Christian was that it was possible for a person to be a Christian and a racist at the same time. Granted, such a racist Christian would not be a complete Christian, but a professing Christian nevertheless.

Our oldest daughter graduated from the high school attached to the Christian university where I taught. During those years we had adjusted to very severe rules and regulations regarding dating and social activities. Everything was chaperoned, and no one, absolutely no one, was trusted to be alone with a member of the opposite sex.

It was within this context that a senior boy at the high school asked Laurie for a date. We had no objection, because we knew Emilio to be a young man with a strong Christian testimony and an excellent reputation. His father was a physician in Mexico, and the entire family were known to be solid Christians.

As was always the case in this legalistic institution, permission had to be granted for dating, and if the school was opposed, the feelings of the families involved mattered not in the least.

Laurie was told that she and Emilio could not date.

Why? Emilio had identified himself on his application as a Mexican, and because of this he and Laurie were not allowed to date. No "interracial" dating was allowed. As if to soften the blow, Laurie and Emilio were told that if Emilio had identified himself simply as an American, no one would have questioned his "race," and he and Laurie could have dated. But, if he had identified himself as an American, he would not have been allowed to date any of the Mexican or other Latin American girls on the campus.

Now all this makes perfect sense to a legalist, regardless of how bizarre it may seem to others. Consistency is a virtue for legalistic Christians, even if the consistency applies to something as bigoted and arrogant as the racism I have just described. On this legalistic campus, Japanese were not allowed to date Chinese, Filipinos could not date Vietnamese, and "Americans" could not date Mexicans. Galatians 3:28 was rarely quoted on this campus, and for good reason. The apostle Paul felt the need to remind the Galatian church that "There is neither Jew nor Greek, there is neither bond nor free, there is neither male nor female: for ye are all one in Christ Jesus."

All one in Jesus, perhaps, but certainly not in legalism.

Error 4: The Halo Effect

The halo effect describes the tendency to let some positive or negative characteristic bias one's overall impression of a person. A halo conveys the idea that there is a "surrounding impression" of a person based on whether that person is liked, accepted, has credentials, is recommended, or otherwise "certified" as being "safe."

Consequently, legalistic Christians, already prone to isolation and suspicion, tend to overvalue the importance of "reports" about people. In applying for a job in a legalistic ministry, as I did for the university job, a recommendation from my pastor was absolutely essential. Otherwise the administration of the university would not have had a "halo" to help them decide whether to hire me.

This obviously leads to some very poor decisions, because people have all kinds of reasons for recommending or not recommending someone for consideration, and it is as likely that good people will be overlooked because of their "halo" as that unacceptable people will be hired because of theirs.

The next step is that once the halo is in place the person may be overvalued, for no other credentials are needed. This overvaluing of people considered to be safe is a kind of spiritual inbreeding that leads to mutations not unlike those known to occur when blood relatives conceive children. This process also helps explain why the more retreatist Christians make such peculiar public statements at times. The leaders are reinforced by members who have placed the "halo" around them. A chancellor of a legalistic Christian university called the wife of the president of the United States a "slut" because of the position she took on an issue. A reluctant and pious-sounding apology eventually was issued, one that was well known to be as insincere as the original comment was un-Christian.

Why would a respectable Christian leader resort to such unkind characterizations of the wife of a public official? Because calling people names is a natural consequence of the mental labeling and categorizing typical of legalism.

Some of the more legalistic Christian churches and colleges are strongly "anti-Pope" because of his "arrogance" of presuming to speak for all Catholics. In reality, however, legalistic churches and colleges are usually headed by their own version of a "Protestant Pope" who presumes to speak for all "their own" people in the same manner. Each time a Jonestown-type scandal comes before the public eye, it involves a religious leader described as "charismatic" who convinced "his" people to accept his words even when Scripture itself is contradicted.

The halo effect applied to the present state of Christian legalism helps explain why "cloistered" groups who stay to themselves and only listen to their own leaders seem to be so sure that they are correct and everyone else is living in gross doctrinal error. Whether this is called retreatism, barricade mentality, or just extreme legalism, the effect is to keep people from the joy of fellowship with other believers, a major benefit of becoming a Christian in the first place.

Error 6: Attribution

To attribute means to make up a reason where none exists. A person assumes to know why something happened, why someone did or said something, and even why someone became a victim of another's actions. To attribute is to assume that one's own perspective is correct. Everyone attributes cause and motive sometimes to some extent because all are human, but legalistic Christians take their attributions too seriously and make significant decisions based on them.

Legalists will boldly proclaim that "anyone" behaving in a certain way outside the narrow limits of legalistic boundaries must be lost, reprobate, or misguided. "Anyone" associating with a leader of another denomination or religious persuasion "must" be deluded by the devil himself, because "no right thinking Christian" would do such a thing. Recall the legalist's logic that no one who is a "true Christian" would behave in such a manner or associate with such people.

Legalistic Christians go even further in assuming that they know not only the behavior and associations of the person under suspicion but also the environmental and situational factors. Remember that legalistic Christians believe that isolation from the world is the best protection against sin, and when a person behaves in a way that is unacceptable to the legalist, it is not the situation or circumstances that need to be taken into consideration but the very state of the person's spirituality.

I have a friend who for several years worked on the vice squad of his precinct. Roland was a solid Christian with a good testimony, married for many years to Lorrain, and the father of three boys. Linda and I had become friends with them and invited them to our married couples Sunday school class. They eventually joined the church and Sunday school class and continued there for many years.

I had nominated Roland for the deacon board in the church and was asked to speak with the pastor about him before he was considered. This was a legalistic church with no divorced people in the choir, all members of the church staff graduates of the same legalistic Christian university, no beards or moustaches on deacons, and so on. The standard legalistic "package."

The pastor and I talked about Roland for some time and then he dropped the bombshell on me. "Dave," the pastor said, "haven't you ever wondered *why* Roland works on the vice squad of the police department?"

Now I had just assumed that it was because Roland was a moral person and wanted to help clean up his area of the city, no small task, obviously. But my legalistic pastor had made a totally different "attribution." He assumed that this Christian police officer was suspect because of the occupational choice he had made.

"Why would Roland choose a job that brings him into daily contact with the worst kind of sin? Dave, I am worried that if we accept Roland as a deacon, people will wonder about him and why he is on our deacon board."

Back to appearances again. I should have known better. Roland was rejected because the pastor assumed there must be a sinister reason for his occupational choice. Though unsaid, I believe the pastor was convinced that Roland had chosen this area of work so it would bring him into contact with sin, regardless of how exemplary Roland's testimony was.

Christians outside the legalistic barricades cannot win on this one. Legalistic Christians will always assume they know why other people act as they do, and they are not restrained by facts or Christian trust.

Error 7: Faulty Logic

I can recall spending time in what then seemed to be fruitless explorations into something our high school social studies teacher called logic. We had a lot of fun playing around with what our teacher seemed to take so seriously. He went to great lengths to explain that something may seem logical yet be totally untrue and impossible. The examples we came up with for our version of logic went something like this:

My dog likes pizza.
Your girlfriend likes pizza.
Therefore, your girlfriend must be a dog.

Okay, so high school humor leaves something to be desired, but such silly logic finds a comfortable home in the legalistic Christian community.

Legalistic versions of high school logic are seen in the tendency to assume that because a person has one characteristic (likes contemporary Christian music, for example) that person will have the other "logical" characteristics (long hair, sexy clothing, etc.) that are "assumed" to go along with it. The most common variety of legalistic logic has to do with the ubiquitous word *compromise*, a catchall term that has only negative connotations for the Christian legalist.

The error of logic that so distinguishes legalistic Christians shows itself in virtually every area of their lives. The error encompasses friends and family, strangers, and other Christians. To be called a compromiser is the ultimate insult for a legalist, because it removes a person from fellowship and theological credibility.

For example, see the likely logic that would lead Christian legalists to say in response to this book, "Well, we always knew Miller was a compromiser."

I will be called a compromiser because I challenge the legitimacy of the legalistic position; because I make this challenge, the "logical" legalistic assumption will be that I am not even really a Christian, because no Christian would write such things about other Christians, would he? The logic will be something like this:

People who challenge us cannot really be Christians.
Dave Miller is challenging us.
Therefore, Dave Miller cannot be a "real" Christian.
Anyone who is not a "real" Christian is a compromiser.
Therefore, Dave Miller is a compromiser.

I remind myself that *nothing* can separate us from the love of God, not even the labels, accusations, or logic of others.

There are some obvious similarities between errors of logic and attributional errors, but the differences are important, too. The distinction between errors of logic and errors of attribution can be seen in the impact each has on people.

Errors of attribution tend to be limited to one person at a time in a given situation, such as to my friend Roland on the police force. Errors of logic tend to be broader both in their application and in the degree of mind warp experienced by people who make this error.

Logical error is related to the personal character of the target Christian. This error is more dangerous because of the presupposition that once the compromise has been exposed, for example, the entire character of the person is proven to be contaminated. Compromise, logic explains, must by its nature touch every area of a Christian's life and is not limited to the one problem that was first noticed.

Here is another example. If a Christian young person from a legalistic family attending a legalistic church is "exposed" for listening to rock music, logic dictates that this young person *must* be corrupt in other areas, too. When the young person decides to "get right" on an issue like music, legalistic leadership will require confession in all the other "assumed" areas that "must have been contaminated, too." Legalistic leadership, logically but often incorrectly, assumes that music was one element in an inevitable absorption into all manner of other sins.

The Ultimate Result of
Legalistic Errors: Isolation

Isolation is an unavoidable corollary to Christian legalism. Isolation is considered a natural and even desirable way to live, protecting from the contamination of the world. The errors we have examined result from the physical, psychological, and spiritual isolation of legalistic Christians. The isolation of legalism feeds on itself, resulting in ever greater separation.

As with any extreme mindset, a certain amount of deprogramming must take place if recovery is to occur. If success in breaking away from Christian legalism is to happen, it will be based on the unconditional love and acceptance of Christians outside the legalist camp.

The one factor that most moved my family away from legalism was the love and unconditional acceptance by the very people we were supposed to fear and avoid: friends and relatives who did not ridicule the extremism that was so obvious to everyone but those inside its walls; friends and relatives who asked us open-ended questions rather than attacking us as our legalistic leaders said they would. Thank God for those who loved us more than we were allowed to love ourselves, and who valued us enough to be patient with our struggles. Time is of essence in the battle to break free of legalism. We are in our tenth year away from legalism, yet it remains a spiritual and interpersonal issue that arises almost daily.

The battle is worth the price. Retaining personal salvation is not the issue, but happiness and joy that have been shelved in the name of pharisaical piety and "lifestyle purity" are. The Miller family is free of legalism, and the costs involved are well worth the effort. If you feel that you are becoming legalistic, go back to your Bible and read of the *unconditional* love of God and the willingness of Jesus to be in contact with "publicans and sinners."

Nothing can separate us from the love of God.

9

Psycho-Spiritual Aspects of Legalism

U p to this point I have looked primarily at the manifestations of legalism among Christian families. I have used examples of families and individuals known to me personally and professionally who have suffered under the yoke of legalism. I trust these real experiences have been helpful in describing the nature of legalism and the damage it can do to a Christian family.

I turn now to a more psychological explanation of how legalism works its way into family life. Applying some of the principles of psychology—what my legalistic, extreme-fundamentalist friends call the evil science—will add to the understanding that informed Christians need to recognize the problem and become healing agents.

The Psychological Framework

A locus is a place or a center at which all points converge. It may be compared to a center of gravity. Or, it is the fulcrum point such as on a seesaw, the center of balance that limits variations in movement but also allows a smaller child to lift a heavier child.

Psychologists speak of the locus (or seat) of control and the locus (or seat) of responsibility of an individual. They are centers or location points at which the person finds both a reason for an action or belief and a way to either accept or reject responsibility for that action or belief. A person believes his or her locus of control is either internal (inside of self) or external (outside of self) and believes the locus of responsibility to be either internal or external.

All persons have these two loci. No one is exclusively internally or externally centered or motivated; however, psychologists do find that everyone is primarily one or the other.

Christians have a particular interest in the concept of locus of control and locus of responsibility. They profess their locus of control to be the Holy Spirit, that person of the godhead who whispers to warn and encourage the individual believer. And Christians profess their locus of responsibility to be their own grace-filled lives, their acceptance of the unconditional love of God as revealed in his Word and confirmed in their experience.

Internal Control

Christians with an internal locus of control accept that what happens to them is primarily the result of their own actions. Rather than tell God, "The devil made me do it," internally controlled Christians know that while the devil may lay temptation in the pathway, no one forces them to stop and look at that temptation, much less decide to pick it up and take it home. They assume that what they do wrong is no one's fault but their own. They control what they do, and recognize that once they place themselves in the place of temptation and sin, heading down a road with no exit ramps, they alone have chosen which road to travel.

Internally controlled Christians tend to be willing to challenge the situation and environment and are less prone to be afraid of what a mistake or wrong action might cause. Such Christians tend to be less anxious than others because they have higher real trust in the guidance of the Holy Spirit in their lives as well as know better what they are individually capable of accomplishing. Frequently this lower level of anxiety results in a higher level of motivation and achievement. Typically optimistic rather than pessimistic, the internally controlled Christian thinks through a problem more carefully and accurately and generally reaches a more suitable answer.

Internally controlled Christians, then, are accepting of the work of the Holy Spirit in their lives while at the same time cognizant of their own degree of control over what they do. Being internally controlled, such Christians do not tend to be conformist in their attitudes, but rather have confidence in the value of their own tastes, desires, and judgments as defined by the guidance of the Holy Spirit.

External Control

Christians whose locus of control is external depend on external forces such as circumstances, powerful people, or world events to control them. They "blow with the wind" whose source is whatever authority outside themselves they have allowed to rule them, whether that authority be good or evil. They are not in control of their own destiny; rather, they believe it is dominated by outside forces or persons. Hence, they would rather pray than prepare when trouble comes.

Externally controlled Christians also assume that rewards and punishments occur independently of their own actions. They are typically uncomfortable with such feelings of weakness, and to reduce their discomfort convince themselves that the bad things happening to them are due in fact to "evil forces" rather than anything they might have done. For example, a bad experience such as financial setback or unemployment is blamed on the devil or what the world calls luck.

If not the devil, then other people are the cause of whatever happens. We previously saw this as attribution: When an answer to hard-to-explain human behavior is needed but unavailable, one is made up and attributed to someone else. Externally controlled persons have little confidence in (and possibly little recognition of) their own inner strengths or creative thoughts. They are thus insecure in themselves and look to outside factors for security. For this they are very attracted to conforming to other people's practices or standards. They are willing to let other people decide for them.

It must also be added that such Christians profess that their external locus of control is God, not an easily arguable point for any Christian. However, the God of the externally controlled Christian tends to be fatalistic and punitive, not quite a reliable and complete source of unconditional love and fountain of human joy.

Legalism offers what these Christians want and need.

Internal Responsibility

It generally follows that Christians whose locus of control is within themselves also take the responsibility to act and feel responsible for the results or consequences of their actions. This internal responsibility grows out of their internal security and confidence in the ability to make their own choices that was created in them and in their security in God's forgiving love.

This confidence does not imply an arrogance in such Christians, however. In fact, they tend to give credit where credit is due but not to blame other persons or circumstances or events for adversities in their own lives. If there is any danger in being this type of person it is to acquire a burden of too much self-blame. Sometimes it becomes impossible for such persons to carry the entire responsibility burden alone, and a physical and spiritual weariness sets in until the Christian in this state releases the burden to Jesus.

Occasionally such an overburdened Christian finds relief or escape in legalism. In legalism adherence to limitations and rules diffuses personal responsibility, spreads it around and onto externals. Unfortunately, this does not usually lead to greater dependence on the strength of the Lord.

External Responsibility

Because the externally controlled Christian believes that what happens to self or family in this life is more a result of outside forces than one's inner control or choices, it follows that this allows an escape from responsibility. Responsibility lies outside that person.

Psychologists call a person whose locus of responsibility is external a system-blame person. Such persons believe that ultimate responsibility for their actions or beliefs falls at the feet of other people or circumstances. A system blamer sees the world as a hostile place and approaches people with suspicion and mistrust. He or she is always and by nature looking for a scapegoat on which to place his or her burden of responsibility. Legalism fills this person's need by providing labels and categorizing the outsiders who are convenient objects of blame.

This, too, makes a very dependent person: Someone else has to act first, make decisions, dream up the ideas, take responsibility, and lead. Legalism fills this person's needs by providing authoritarian leaders who are all too willing to accept this delegated responsibility.

Control, Responsibility, and Legalism

Clearly, individuals whose locus of control is external also tend to have an external locus of responsibility and will be attracted to the more legalistic forms of Christianity. Because they believe their lives are basically in the hands of others, putting themselves in the hands of a group that fortifies itself against the "evil others" of the rest of the world affords the best hope of security.

But the internally controlled and internally responsible Christians offer us a more optimistic picture, providing examples of Christian maturity. While acknowledging both personal choice and personal responsibility, they trust in the God who made them and believe in the protective power of the God who created his people so they could love him by choice and not by force. They do not need the protection of legalism, because they have the strength of God within them in the person of the Holy Spirit. And they have the joy of belonging to the whole family of God.

Developmental Stages In and Out of Legalism

We have defined the psychological types of personalities that are most likely to be drawn to Christian legalism. However, we know that in real life individuals and circumstances vary greatly. Anyone can be drawn into legalism. Just as none are born Christian, none are born legalistic. Something happens to start the process.

I offer the following five stages people generally go through in the legalizing process to help readers recognize what can happen and to encourage those who are taking steps to move out of legalism.

I will relate in the next few pages some personal and family experiences to illustrate what can and does happen to Christian individuals and families. I neither pretend to know all there is to know about this process nor assert that what I am about to relate covers all situations and all varieties of Christian experience. Nor do I blame anyone but ourselves. Hindsight is clear, however, and we now see that in our eagerness to serve the Lord we loved to the best of our abilities we allowed this to happen to us. Only after many years did we come to know better.

Stage 1: Entry and Enmeshment

In the beginning was salvation!

This is the almost universal experience of those who wind up in a legalistic Christian environment. The process begins with individual salvation or the salvation of one's parents. Most new converts are strongly and correctly encouraged to become formally involved in a good, Bible-believing church in their area.

In the case of the Miller family (at the time Linda and I and Linda's parents), we were invited to a solid fundamentalist church with a good reputation in a growing suburb of the large metropolitan area where we lived. We had been converted to biblical Christianity at a very large church but did not feel very comfortable there. In the church we chose we were made welcome and quickly became members, were baptized, and remained there for the next fourteen years. Linda and I served as adult class group leaders in the early Sunday school and regular teachers in the later Sunday school. I ushered at all services in church, we regularly visited on Thursday nights, Linda worked in the nursery and we felt totally at home.

This was *our* church!

But slowly we were being drawn into legalism without being aware that it was happening. We loved our pastor and still do, but we were being taught the basic premises of legalism, namely, to evaluate people on the basis of appearance and behavior, and to fix a spiritual level using the measure of conformity to a set of extra-biblical rules and regulations. Being a good Christian, we were taught, is based on what is in a person's heart but is always evident by outward behavior.

Consequently, no male in our church choir grew a beard or moustache. Ushers had to adhere to the same set of appearance standards as choir members. Nursery workers wore skirts regardless of the difficulties involved in wearing that attire while caring for toddlers and babies. Church sponsored activities had to conform to a dress code to insure that the church would not be wrongly perceived because of someone's shorts or other "immodest" dress. On one occasion our adult Sunday school class had to cancel an evening of fellowship at a local restaurant because the owners had obtained a liquor license in the previous days without telling the church; because we could not be "seen" around alcohol we had to call it off at the last minute.

I realize these may seem either trivial or just silly to the reader. But the issue is not what was happening so much as the underlying principle. As young Christians we were being discipled by people who really loved us and cared about our welfare, but we were also being taught that our place in the church family was tenuous and could easily be lost through bad behavior, or as church leadership would often say, behavior that would "embarrass" our Lord.

But we were happy in that church, which continues to be a light for the Lord in that community to this day, though our pastor has retired and been replaced by a much younger man. Then in 1975, the Lord called the Miller family into full-time Christian service. We thought the mission field would be where we would wind up, and after applying to our mission board we were directed to get a year's Bible training at a Bible school somewhere before we went to the field. I had a B.S. and an M.Ed. in education and counseling by that time, and Linda had finished nursing school and was a new R.N.

Because the entire staff of our home church was from one Christian college (typical of legalistic churches), we were encouraged to apply there and were accepted. I resigned my position as an assistant principal with the city's public school system, we sold our house, and we were on our way.

When we arrived at the college, I was informed that my part-time teaching job could be expanded to full time due to the sudden departure of one of the psychology professors. Financial pressures were greater than we had anticipated, so I took the full-time position. It became a six-year position because of some closed doors on the mission field. Linda was a nurse in the hospital's obstetrical unit. We were happy to be there, and decided that the Lord in his wisdom had changed our area of service from foreign missions to college students. We continue to serve Christian education to this day.

Over the years during this stage we had learned to become discriminatory Christians, feeling we were better than those in "liberal" denominations and conventions and that Christians like us were better than any other "variations" of Christian. No matter that the others might hold *exactly* the same doctrinal position on all the "fundamentals" of the Christian faith, their lifestyles, clothing, haircuts, or Christian colleges made them second-class Christians in our minds. It was all we had known up to that point.

We loved our own group and not many others, and we were constantly reinforced for being correctly "separated" Christians. Years later, we learned that the members of Linda's family who had faithfully witnessed to us and actually led us to the Lord had become very concerned about the cultic quality of the Christianity we were then living.

Stage 2: Dissonance

Very slowly the Holy Spirit was convicting us that we were being too exclusive in our Christian fellowship and alienating the very people who loved us and were our spiritual parents.

During the first stage of enmeshment we had become discriminatory, elitist, reclusive, and arrogant, a difficult thing for me to admit. But the Lord was not going to abandon us to legalism. We were beginning to turn the corner and though there were going to be some difficult "birthing" pains ahead of us, we were on the road to being recovering Christian legalists. We began entering the second stage of legalism: dissonance.

Though Linda and I were beginning our movement out of legalism, we did not at that time understand how the Lord was working this out for us. It took many years of repetitive teaching to make us separated, elitist, and arrogant, and it was not going to be an easy process of change.

Change was first manifested in our feelings of discomfort with some of the things we were hearing. Still, we were fully involved, giving total commitment and submission to the leadership of this institution, being as "full-time" as it was possible to be.

We could not articulate why we began to feel uncomfortable. Thinking back, I can liken that feeling to the way the Lord had first convicted Linda and me to give ourselves for full-time Christian ministry. The Lord worked on each of us separately, without our discussing it with each other. We waited several months before either of us brought it up. Then, at that point we were astounded at how the Lord had been leading each of us in exactly the same direction. We had been so indoctrinated into the importance of being loyal to church, or in this case Christian college, we had become reluctant to raise this issue with each other even in the privacy of our own home.

We really don't remember who brought up the "strange feelings" we had been having about the place we were serving, but this was the dissonance that characterizes the second stage of transition. We were experiencing conflict between what we were being told in church and chapel services and the values we had grown up with. The institution's racial bigotry was beginning to bother us most. This and others were extra-biblical issues rather than doctrinal matters, but in that institution such issues took on the full weight of doctrine.

Our attitude at that time was one of self-doubt about whether we had really understood what the Lord wanted us to do. We were torn between our feelings of loyalty for the institution and our rising sense of discomfort with the content of sermons and chapel messages castigating not only atheists but also Catholics, Jews, Southern Baptists, charismatics, and virtually every other variety of religious experience one can think of except hyperfundamentalism.

Linda and I had long discussions on whether or not we really agreed with what we were hearing more and more frequently, and we were becoming concerned with the increasingly isolated and radical direction this form of modern Christianity was taking. The very big issue at the time—race relations—made us feel more and more like strangers in this place. Linda and I had been raised to be nonracist and it seemed for a time there that every other chapel message or sermon was aimed at emphasizing "racial purity." We knew we were in the minority.

Thus we reached extreme discomfort over what seemed to us to be antagonistic, unloving, bigoted, and chauvinistic attitudes of the leaders of this institution coupled with their absolute lack of scriptural support for their extreme positions and their unwillingness to discuss these positions with "subordinates." This second stage covered about two years, and we realized that our tenure in that ministry would be limited.

Stage 3: Resistance

By approximately four years into our service in this particular institution, not only were Linda and I increasingly uncomfortable with the radical direction of the institution, particularly its growing public position on total separation of the races and obvious attitudes of "beneficent superiority" of its leadership, but we were becoming somewhat suspect in the minds of the authority figures administering the college.

We cared more and more about how our minority students felt about this particular manifestation of Christianity and what it was doing to our children. We had to support the institution's policy of no dating between races to our children even though we did not and do not hold this position; yet it was a condition of our employment to support it.

We tried to ask questions in as respectful a manner as possible, but as is so often the case with legalistic organizations, any questioning was assumed to imply disloyalty and even spiritual failure. We also found that the more questions we raised (always on nondoctrinal issues, remember) the more we were criticized and the more our children were suspect as well. Legalistic Christians typically believe that an expressed attitude on the part of one family member reflects the thinking of the entire family. After all, we were reminded, can two walk together except they be agreed?

This suspicion leveled against our older children helped convince us that the Lord was preparing our pathway out of legalism.

Stage 4: Personal and Spiritual Introspection

It should be obvious that we were going through a very difficult time of personal and spiritual re-evaluation. Stages three and four were not pleasant experiences for the Miller family, though the end result once again confirmed the grace of God in all these matters.

Because of the controversy surrounding some of the issues being taken by this particular institution and the bold defense by its leadership, it was inevitable that we would wonder if maybe we were the ones in error on these issues. Perhaps what had been implied to us in response to our concern with the direction of the institution was true. Perhaps we were simply wrong in challenging God-ordained leadership. Perhaps we were out of step with the progress of modern Christianity.

After much prayer and thoughtful consideration Linda and I reached the point at which we felt very comfortable with our own beliefs about race, separation, fellowship and such and were forced to acknowledge that which we had so strongly resisted up to that point: that we did not belong in the ministry where we were serving.

We just could not bring ourselves to believe that there were no other Christians serving God and living right except our small group and a few of the graduates of this institution. In six years of four-a-week chapel services, we heard not one word in support of other Christian schools, the graduates of other schools, or churches who did not blindly follow the prescriptions and proscriptions of this university. We could no longer pretend to believe that the only truly faithful and correct Christians in the entire world were at this institution and a few "colonies" around the world led by its graduates. We could no longer accept the rejection of any other form of worship, church music, choir robes, or lifestyle simply because it differed from what was practiced in one locality.

We loved the people in the university, but we did not love the extrascriptural teachings that were more and more radical and inconsistent with the traditional fundamentals of the faith. We had never prayed so hard about anything up to that point in time. We were asking for nothing more than leadership from the Holy Spirit, and we remain grateful to God that that leadership was supplied. Though the actual change was not going to be easy, we were stepping out onto the highway that would lead us away from legalism and in the direction of genuine love.

Stage 5: Exit

So six years after our entry into institutional legalism (as distinct from the milder form of legalism practiced in our home church) we moved out. The school had become increasingly worried about the direction of my concerns and decided not to renew my teaching contract for the next year. To be honest, I didn't feel the time was exactly right for a change so I fought the decision. This was without success, of course, and looking back I can see that this was one more way the Lord used to convince me that we needed to be someplace else. I cannot go into detail on this one matter for fear of hurting those still at the school who supported me; suffice it to say that the Lord supplied me with a teaching contract at another Christian college within one month of the decision not to have me back for the next school year.

We involved the children in the decision to move and were impressed with their spiritual maturity in understanding my position as father and head of the family. That last semester was extremely difficult. People we had known for six years no longer spoke to us. One or two of the older children's teachers took them to task, and at one point one of the high school faculty members reminded our senior daughter that her graduation could be disrupted if her dad made waves.

The absence of Christian love from some was outstanding, but the continuing friendship of many others helped us and convinced us that we were not alone in our concern for the direction of this extremely fundamentalist legalist institution.

The Lord gave Linda and me a new ministry in a non-legalistic, doctrinally sound, fundamental/evangelical Christian university. We have been here since 1981 and have seen nothing that would move us away. Now we see the loving and nonjudgmental Christianity we missed all those years without really knowing what it was we were missing. The Lord has confirmed our decision by expanding our ministry and by giving us a peace of heart and mind that Satan could not counterfeit.

For what I have here written I accept total responsibility before God—for its truthfulness and lack of intent to injure anyone. My one desire in making this difficult personal confession is to help others who may be experiencing something similar. For me and for them the grace of God is sufficient.

10

The Bondage of Legalism

Why would anyone want to be a legalist? Why would a Christian trade liberty and the joy of freedom for a mess of extrabiblical rules and regulations? It just doesn't seem to make sense. Wouldn't it be easier and more pleasant to accept the unconditional love of God instead of becoming negative and suspicious of self and others?

We have seen that the answers to these questions are complex. While we have examined the basics of legalism in previous chapters, common sense tells us that every individual has a slightly different set of reasons for being attracted to legalism or for staying in it if having entered as a member of a legalistic family. To understand Christian legalists and the unique qualities of the people behind the rules and regulations, we looked at their upbringing and their personalities in terms of self-concept, attitudes and values, thought processes, emotional balance and expression, and interpersonal behavior.

155

In this chapter we shall take another look to try to tie it all together and see if we can come to conclusions as to what God would want us to know to be able at some point to help a fellow Christian who struggles to break free of the entrapments of legalism.

The Legalistic Personality

Legalistic people share certain characteristics that set them apart from others. Others possess personality traits that would virtually guarantee their protection against legalism: independence, innovative thoughts, creativity, curiosity, and confidence in both God and self. An occasional person will possess these characteristics and be drawn into a legalistic church or educational institution, but likely will not stay for very long.

Conformity

Every legalist is a conformist. Every legalist.

The conformist personality fits into legalism very well because legalists are always in a majority *in the system in which they operate.* Even though legalistic Christians may take a bold public stance on an issue such as abortion, the group to which the conforming legalists belong and from whom they draw support is invariably in agreement with that stance.

The boldest confrontation in recent days is Operation Rescue led by Randall Terry, the most aggressive and forceful assault on the pro-abortion elements since the 1973 *Roe v. Wade* decision legalizing abortion on demand. The leadership and primary organizers of this movement are for the most part good Christian men and women who have only the best Christian qualities of character.

But many in this and other similar "pro-moral" groups would not be there if there were not the massive numbers with whom they could feel safe and secure. I believe the people from legalistic backgrounds would be the first to bail out of the movement if the great numbers of fellow protesters were to diminish.

Conformists struggle when asked to stand alone, and many fail. But even those who succeed will invariably return home following the protest or confrontation to a supportive church and family, the only way a legalist is useful to a movement like Operation Rescue.

Conformity has many sources, and generalizations are the best we can do when examining it at this level. Just as a person may be born into a legalistic Christian family and thereby "inherit" legalistic tendencies, so a person may be born to parents manifesting conformist personalities and thereby learn conformist traits such as intense preoccupation with image and appearance, a need to check things out before stating a position, and great feelings of inferiority and insecurity when challenged even slightly.

Conformist Intelligence

Tracing this conformist personality invariably involves questions of intelligence as well. Child development experts know that high control and strict discipline at home coupled with the presence of a superior-inferior persons structure tends to produce children who are quiet, well behaved, and nonresistant but also limited in curiosity, originality, and imagination. To develop fully functional personalities and thought processes, children must be provided with oppositional elements to confront. In other words, children who are allowed or required to make decisions as they grow up will tend to develop greater ability to think independently compared with those who have had all or most of their important decisions made for them.

Intelligence is not necessarily a factor in predicting a conforming or nonconforming personality. Some think that conformists tend toward the mid- to low-average scale of intelligence, but such speculation has never been verified. The reasons for this speculation are worth considering, though.

Christian legalists are more likely to be conformists—yielding to group pressure. A person of higher intelligence would be more resistant to the attractions of both conformity and legalism because of the higher levels of creativity and risk taking common to those with higher levels of intelligence.

Conforming legalists are fearful of being ridiculed or criticized and are, therefore, strict adherents to the "jot and tittle" while doubting anyone who refers more to the "spirit" of the rule than the wording. Among legalistic Christians, anyone who defends paying more attention to the spirit than the letter of a rule is immediately under suspicion. Legalistic Christians choose slavish obedience to extra-scriptural restrictions such as hair length on men and social associations because such clear-cut, black-and-white, *nonambiguous* issues are easier to understand and deal with. Christian legalists think in this limited, restricted way because they are afraid to risk the unproven.

Authority Worship

Conformists are vulnerable to becoming legalistic, and legalistic Christians will always prove to be conformists. But what may be perceived as conformity or lower levels of original thinking may actually be fear-based reluctance to take a stand. Such a person may have been so thoroughly indoctrinated with "authority worship" that it is exceptionally difficult to go against any position favored by a single authority figure or religious system.

As I prepared to write this book and tell of my experiences in Christian legalism, I was reluctant to include some of the examples you have already read about for fear that a Christian inexperienced with legalism would not believe such things really go on in legalistic systems. I hope you understand that everything you have read really did happen, as did the following story about fear of authority.

You already know of the need for legalistic leadership in churches and colleges and universities to control as many aspects of the lives of "participants" as they can get away with. Many churches, Christian educational institutions, and other kinds of parachurch organizations are known for promoting and living legalism and are famous for inventing rules on everything imaginable from whom and when students may date to how church members must dress and with whom they may fellowship.

One Christian university is famous for its brand of legalism, and the leadership has always taken pride in "out legalizing" other legalistic organizations. Remember that to a legalist, adherence to rules and regulations equates with spirituality, and so the more rules an organization has and the more strictly they are enforced, the more spiritual that organization presumes itself to be.

As students and faculty filed into chapel one weekday they found they would have a visiting pastor for chapel speaker. None of the faculty knew much about this person except that he was known as a pastor who actually instructed deacons to seat women whose skirt length was "too revealing" in specially reserved pews at the back of their sanctuary.

Once introduced as a "faithful supporter of this university and a true friend of real fundamentalists" (emphasis on *real*), he quickly proceeded to his sermon on "behaving Christian" and began a tirade against "hippie hairstyles on boys." No matter that the term *hippie* had been outdated for a decade, and no matter that there wasn't a male within earshot with hair over the ears or collar, this was *his* opportunity to straighten everybody out.

"And not only is long hair on boys ungodly," he shouted, but any "boy" who would part his hair in the middle was "either an active or future homosexual."

"That's right," he continued, "show me a boy with hair parted down the middle and I'll show you a sissy."

There were a few nervous giggles from the audience of about six thousand high school and college students and disbelieving looks between faculty members, but the message proceeded and chapel was dismissed.

You would imagine this would generate discussion and much objection on campus. But there was not a word from the leadership in succeeding chapels about this incredible message. Faculty was quietly informed that the leadership would *never* challenge another Christian who was speaking what he thought to be "revealed" truth.

Although the speaker was a Christian he brought to mind the words of Jesus: "But in vain do they worship me, teaching for doctrines the commandments of men" (Matt. 15:9). This misguided man would be allowed to continue to speak to Christians on his radical ideas sowing all manner of harm, simply because legalistic authority figures were unwilling to publicly challenge another Christian authority figure.

What a travesty!

Emotions and the Legalist

Emotions are scary to the legalistic Christian because they are so difficult to control. The Bible tells that the tongue reveals the thoughts of the "heart," and when a legalist is pressed or stressed, the true feelings come flowing out in such an honest way that a loss of control is experienced. Emotions are the most difficult of human attributes to falsify, too, and legalistic Christians, as always, are consumed with appearances and how they are perceived by others; this, too, results in fear that the "real person" will show through all the legalistic camouflage.

It is because of this fear that legalistic Christians tend to be so easily threatened by any kind of honest emotional expression. Over and over again, students at legalistic Christian secondary schools and colleges and universities are warned of the dangers of "unbridled emotions," though rarely do they hear much on the subject of legitimate or "bridled" emotions. If persons fear themselves because of the emotions that lie unconfronted within them, their entire self-concepts will inevitably suffer.

When confronted on emotions, the legalist retreats behind his or her legalistic beliefs rather than face the challenge. Virtually the only safe emotional expression is through preaching and contact sports.

Faculty at legalistic universities experience pressures equal to or in excess of those experienced by faculty members at secular institutions. When I arrived as a faculty member at a legalistic Christian university I was invited to join the Thursday night faculty-staff basketball league.

If there ever was a person whose body was not suited to basketball it is I. But I wanted to get to know my colleagues and appreciated an opportunity to get some exercise.

There were about ten teams chosen at random in the league. I had a pretty good time until I came face to face with the "dirty doctor" on the basketball court. Just a few minutes into the game, I got elbowed by this top member of the administration of the university. The big shot fouled me and he got away with it!

There is no exaggeration here. This honorary "doctor" was probably the most important person on campus. And the referee acted as though he didn't notice a thing, even though I knew he had seen the foul.

Well, okay, so the ref missed one. Back to the game. A few minutes later, the "dirty doctor" committed a blatant foul on a layup, really creamed the guy, but at least he got called for it this time. Two foul shots and back to action.

Boom! Another cheap shot foul. What in the world was going on here? The big shot was playing dirty, fouling left and right, and getting called only once in a while.

We lost the game.

Later, after the showers, I asked the fellow who had invited me to the team about the fouling.

"Yeah," he said, "sorry about that. I was hoping we wouldn't have to play that team so early in the season."

"So what's the story?" I asked, hoping for something that would make me feel less like a peasant in a feudal kingdom being forced to put up with the whims and excesses of the authoritarian ruler.

"Well," he explained, "We all know that Dr. _____ is under a lot of pressure, and we kind of look the other way and let him blow off a little steam in these games. After all, he really can't let people on the outside see how he really feels, can he?"

I got it!

Because this legalistic authority figure was constrained to keep his honest emotions smothered under a legalistic blanket, he expected faculty and staff to put up with his dirty play during his "recreational times." This very authoritarian leader felt anger and other honest emotions and was unable to express them in a constructive way, so he played dirty with those who really couldn't complain.

What a corruption of honesty and leadership! And all because of the need to "put on a front" and smother emotions under pretense of not having these emotions. Such is the cost of legalism.

The barricade mentality demonstrated in this Christian university leader and so many others leads naturally to the need to find alternative ways of expressing negative emotions such as hostility and anger. What happens when an individual Christian becomes upset with a religious authority figure? If loyalty is an essential element in a Christian's credo, it is unlikely that that Christian will do the right thing and confront that authority figure directly.

But what becomes of the feelings? What comes of the sense of hurt over what the church, school, or leader did?

Usually that emotion is indirectly expressed and targets for retribution are subconsciously chosen, targets that will probably not strike back. Of course, this process will only create more negative emotion in the person chosen to receive the undeserved "nasties," then that person will choose a person to displace his anger, and on the spiral grows.

What characterizes legalistic Christians in the area of emotional functioning is vulnerability to perceived outside threat, being fragile under stress, absence of emotional spontaneity, the displacement of anger and hostility onto defenseless targets (like basketball players), and much higher levels of anxiety. These factors feed off each other like a nuclear reactor feeds off plutonium rods, and the spiral of unmanageability gets bigger and bigger, leading to more suffering all down the line.

I believe this is what can happen when a once-spiritual leader falls into moral sin. As he becomes successful in his ministry and comes in front of the public eye more and more, the pressure to *perform* grows along with a greater need for self-control. Some of these men apparently cannot deal with the pressure, and seek a "secret" way to release the emotional pressure. The sexual component in most of the scandals involving Christian leaders in recent years bears this out.

Such Christians are also prone to migraine headaches, stomach ulcers, skin problems such as neurodermatitis, and a host of other less common anxiety-based physical and psychological reactions. Given that eating is a basic way to reduce anxiety, we should not be surprised to find a greater per capita obesity problem in legalistic Christian environments. If you know legalists, you will probably agree with me that there is a distinct shortage of normal-weight pastors and leaders. The tendency is that legalists will be either compulsively thin or overweight, and the wives of the pastors and leaders who bear the brunt of their husbands' anxiety will be the most overweight of all.

Spiritually, Christians in the state I have just described will come to the point of questioning their salvation and wondering what they did that got God so upset with them. If we remember that legalistic Christians have been taught to evaluate the interior of a person by examining the exterior, the natural progression toward ever greater levels of anxiety is obvious. The unconditional love of God is never more hidden than in the life of a legalist under stress.

The Legalist and Self-Concept

Self-concept is no less important to a Christian than to anyone else, though these days any use of the term *self* in relation to a Christian is taken by some to be suspicious. A person's self-concept is based on the level of agreement between what psychologists call the ideal self and the self as realistically experienced.

Legalistic Christians struggle with self-concept because legalism teaches that spirituality is best measured by assessing outward behavior and conformity to a set of standards established by an authority figure. Because such Christians believe they never really measure up to what God and people expect of them, self-concept is typically lower than for nonlegalistic Christians with more reasonable understandings of what is expected of them.

Psychologists and others in the helping professions ascribe the term *fear of failure* to a person excessively hindered in personal growth and development by a fear of failing. When we find Christians in this category they typically are or have been involved in a legalistic system. The fear of failure is basic to the control mechanisms of legalistic systems, and without instilling this fear legalistic leaders would lose some degree of control over "their" people.

Legalistic pastors and other speakers work to convince their members that they have absolutely no chance of winning when they confront evil. Their only chance for victory is to withdraw and stay behind the spiritual barricades of their legalistic church or educational institution and pray for the Lord to return before the devil gets to them. The negativism that so characterizes legalism is intentional on the part of leadership to protect their power but is presented as a crucial way of "protecting" their people from the evil of other less rigid and controlling religious systems.

Stifling Creativity

The scarcity of creative, innovative ideas, theories, and even art forms attests to the control of legalism. The legalistic Christian finds safety and security only in the tried and true. In my twenty years in legalism, I suppose I heard "If it's new it can't be true" hundreds of times, usually followed by a stinging criticism of methods employed by a Christian leader who managed to come up with a fresh approach to some aspect of ministry. The way to avoid being judged negatively by one's legalistic peers is to refrain from taking chances or experimenting with new methods or ideas.

If you can identify a legalistic church, school, or organization in your area—and this is usually easy by just looking at the rules and behavioral restrictions in effect—you will find a scarcity or complete absence of any truly creative works. Christian legalists can be as talented and creative as anyone, of course, but legalism stifles both motivation and opportunity for expression.

Thus there is no avant-garde with legalistic Christians. Only that which has proven successful may be used. No new music is acceptable unless it mimics traditional music forms. Religious ritual, so often attacked by legalistic Christians as godless "liturgy," is actually the common currency of legalism. Visit a legalistic church and return in ten years for another visit and you will find things *exactly* as they were.

New art forms are out of the question, and sculpture that fails to represent the praying hands is worldly. Writing is restricted to "acceptable" topics, rationalized by the need to "educate but not confuse"—buzz words for simple indoctrination. Translated from "legal-ese" this means that Christian authors may rework old story lines and update classics, but genuine new work is going to be suspect. Witness that legalistic colleges and universities seem to quickly develop their own publishing and printing entities, a reflection both of the control that is so important as well as distrust of other Christian publishing houses. Some Christian universities and colleges will not allow faculty to publish other than through their own "house" publishers, and to try to do so is usually grounds for termination.

If John Bunyan were writing *Pilgrim's Progress* today, legalistic Christians would brand it as radical, "new-age oriented," and off limits for "good" Christians.

Legalistic Values and Attitudes

Because of their emphasis on suspecting anything new, legalistic Christians are drawn toward the traditional, conventional, standard way of living. This is no less true of values and attitudes. Legalistic Christians find security in well-established values. The comfort of tested values is the feeling of old, well-worn but comfortable shoes. The difficulty is that shoes like values must be replaced as they wear out or be resoled so they can continue to be useful in new situations.

Legalists soak up traditional values and attitudes like dry sponges, and then rework them into armor to protect their soft, vulnerable spirituality. For personal protection, legalistic Christians must see only in black and white.

Intolerance helps explain why legalistic Christians have such a need to categorize everyone. They can be identified by their questions of and comments about a newly met person. Imagine for a moment you are at a convention of Christians and have just been introduced to a person from a legalistic Christian university or college, one that is known to emphasize separation at all levels. Here are the kinds of comments and questions you will get from a legalist:

"Nice to meet you John. Do you folks live in the area?

"Really! And what church do you attend?

"Hmmm! Isn't that a 'convention' church?

"No? Well, that's good to hear.

"Say, did you attend a Christian college?

"Good for you. Which one?

"Hmm! Isn't that the school started by _____? I

understand he has gotten involved with _____,
the well-known president of_____."

"Well, anyway sure was nice meeting you, John. See you
later."

As John walks away, the legalist turns to his wife standing there and says, "Well, I guess we know where *that* guy
is coming from!"

A little silly, you say? Then you haven't been around
Christian legalists very much. This kind of interrogation
is very common to legalists and is based on that very
important need to categorize that makes them feel safe
and secure. Such folks absolutely must know as much as
possible about a person so ambiguity can be reduced.

Faculty and student body at one large legalistic Christian university were warned by the chancellor to "watch
out for people who just tell you they are Christian. They
are usually trying to hide something."

It is not enough to know that people are fellow believers. The legalist must press on to find out the exact
denominational affiliation of the pastor and church
staff, where they went to school, which seminars and
speakers they invite, and most importantly these days,
where they plan to send their children to college. Once
the legalist has his answers, a decision is made either to
make or break fellowship, and the chances are great that
the decision will be to break fellowship. Legalists are so
burdened down with criteria for fellowship that they
become and more and more isolated and eventually find
themselves back behind the walls with only a few "loy-
alists" for company.

This is bondage, every bit as much as a person being
blackmailed or kept in a prison.

Authoritarian Personality

A major aspect of personal attitudes and values within legalism is submission to authority. This personality type is characterized by a belief in the benefits of subverting personal will to that of a "legitimate" Christian leader. Authoritarian people tend to be good followers, as well as leaders when the situation requires it.

Legalistic churches have authoritarian men for pastors and are rarely "board led." Such churches will be led by a very persuasive pastor who is powerful, rigid, and confident as he alone "leads *his* flock." Such churches will only employ authoritarian men in staff positions, because the authoritarian personality accepts the duty to follow as well as to lead.

The Bible teaches that "as [a man] thinketh in his heart, so is he" (Prov. 23:7), and those following an authoritarian leader need to recognize the internal personality and mind-set of the man with whom they are dealing. Authoritarian pastors and leaders tend to impose their personal preferences on the congregation. It is common for a "cult of the personality" to grow up around such men, leading to excessive loyalty to the man rather than the cause of Christ.

Legalism Begets Legalism

Any form of flexibility is branded compromise by legalists. Any willingness to work with people of a different religious faith is seen as evidence of compromise. Certain legalists, for example, will not get involved in the prolife movement because they see it as dominated by Roman Catholics. No matter that the cause is just, legalists need to avoid "the appearance of evil" by shunning such common labors. The same reluctance to get involved applies to antipornography movements, because there, too, "others" are involved who might not have exactly the right kind of stand on legalistic issues like separation. Only in recent years has this reluctance been overcome in getting conservative Christians to register and vote on certain approved issues.

Interpersonal Relations and Legalism

Legalism puts barriers between people. It should be no surprise that interpersonal relationships will feel the impact of legalism, too.

Because legalists accept the premise that external behavior reflects internal condition, how one is thought of or perceived is of utmost importance. This is compounded by the tendency of legalistic Christians to assume that "acceptable" others are as interested in externals as the legalists are.

Several years ago while the children were still small, Linda came down with a flulike illness that just knocked her flat for a few days. We were deeply involved in a legalistic church then and very careful about appearances.

But this was Sunday night, church night for us, and not only was Linda too ill for church but she needed to have a prescription filled that had been called in to a local pharmacy by our doctor.

What was the problem? I was "supposed" to be in church. I am embarrassed to admit it, but I actually stayed home without the medicine Linda needed until church was over. *Then* I went to the pharmacy for the medicine.

Now, before you tell me how ridiculous I was, remember that legalism teaches its adherents to avoid being "stumbling blocks" to others who "do not have what we have." Legalists refrain from many activities on Sunday and other times when services might be held, not necessarily because they want to do what is right any more than does any other Christian, but because they have been so conditioned to avoid doing wrong. The motivation is skewed, of course, and serious problems can be expected when the kids become teenagers and begin to ask questions Mom and Dad cannot answer.

The preoccupation with appearances tends to corrupt the ability of legalists to "discern" the spiritual condition or personality of others. Mature Christians are supposed to be effective discerners of good and evil, wise as serpents and harmless as doves. Legalistic Christians have smothered their discerning radar in a fog of preoccupation with how *they* will be perceived by others. The consequence of this is a slavish loyalty to authority figures who are all too happy to do their discerning for them.

Untying the Knot

What now?

Now that we have begun to understand the process of legalism and the dangers involved, how can we escape from or avoid altogether this corruption of Gods' love?

I believe we must work at making sure our own families are not ensnared in legalism, and at the same time help to free those already tied up in the cords of legalism. We can facilitate each by praying and by demonstrating the love of God in our own lives. Remember, legalists are looking for love just like the rest of us. But they have been told they have to earn God's love, if they can, and others' approval, and we must help them know that God's love is unconditional. Love changes the heart more efficiently than anything else, even for hard-hearted legalists.

We cannot, as Jesus did, know the inner workings of each heart; therefore we must caution against being simply accusatory. Only love unconditionally. It is Christian love that breaks the bondage of legalism.

Conclusion
Breaking Free

This is not my first book, but it is by far the most difficult and challenging I have written. It was difficult for me to share so many personal experiences. I know I have lost some of our friends in legalism whose legalistic limitations will not allow them to see the message of love in this book. I have had this topic in mind for more than ten years, but I have actively resisted my own desire to explore and verbalize it because of what Linda and I will certainly lose.

What made me write it, then?

It was the anguish and real spiritual turmoil I saw in many good, solid, Bible-believing Christians whose lives are controlled by legalistic authorities. If it were not for the families I have counseled and encouraged to join "Legalists Anonymous" and in turn encouraged me to share these thoughts with as many as possible, this book would not have been written. My life would certainly have been less complicated if I had continued to resist this book.

My title, *Breaking Free,* is appropriate, I believe, because those who have been deeply involved in legalism will be forever in the process of breaking free from this modern perversion of Christianity. Recovering legalists may become freer but not totally free, because the teachings

173

and social pressures will have become a permanent part of them and will remain so as long as they live. The best they can hope for—and this is pretty good—is to be released from the controlling effects of legalism, enabling them to be able to rise a little closer to God and feel the unconditional warmth of his love. They can be directed by God's Spirit rather than a human authority figure. They can learn to love others again, without condition, just as God loves them.

Linda and I are recovering legalists, as are our children to a lesser extent. In recovery we have relearned how to enjoy an unfettered fellowship with everyone of like faith, even those who part their hair down the middle or decide not to put on their pantyhose once in a while. We are free to fellowship with people from denominations we once were taught were ungodly and unworthy of our company. We are free of our once firmly held barricade mentality, free to attack the gates of hell with a bucket of water. We are now free to love our children and each other as unconditionally as God loves his children, love without limit or excuse, love without apology.

I have avoided arguing about the "true meaning" of certain passages of Scripture. As with witnessing to the non-Christian, I believe arguing is futile with legalists. Only love will have effect. Love facilitates freedom, not debate and controversy. A legalist will never be "rationalized" away from legalism but can be loved into being free.

Two factors are indispensable when trying to help a Christian legalist: unconditional love and personal Bible study.

Unconditional love is the "thorn in the side" that moves a person. Unconditional love is the kind of love God shows to us and that Jesus lived. Unconditional love cares what people do, but cares for the people more than their behavior. Unconditional love enables us to separate sin from the sinner and see the person beneath. Unconditional love convicts of hatred, bigotry, arrogance, and isolationism. Unconditional love, mixed with patience, works for these goals and achieves them.

Bible study will help Christians see the extremism of the system that has been oppressing them. Bible study reveals God's attitude about the sins of legalism. Passages such as these will help:

1. Matthew 15:8: "This people draweth nigh unto me with their mouth, and honoreth me with their lips; but their heart is far from me."
2. Matthew 23:1–5: "Then spake Jesus to the multitude, and to his disciples, saying, The scribes and pharisees sit in Moses' seat: All therefore what they bid you observe, that observe and do; but do not ye after their works: for they say, and do not. *For they bind heavy burdens and grievous to be borne, and lay them on men's shoulders;* but they themselves will not move them with one of their fingers. But all their works they do for to be seen of men" (italics added).
3. Luke 11:17: "But he, knowing their thoughts, said unto them, Every kingdom divided against itself is brought to desolation; and a house divided against a house falleth."
4. Luke 15:1–2: "Then drew near unto him all the publicans and sinners for to hear him. And the Pharisees and scribes murmured, saying, This man receiveth sinners, and eateth with them."
5. Matthew 15:9: "But in vain they do worship me, *teaching for doctrines the commandments of men*" (italics added).

I hope this book has helped you as it has helped me to carefully and spiritually consider my own walk with the

Lord now and in my legalistic past. What I have shared with you I have done so in absolute truth; only the names and circumstances were changed to protect the innocent (and sometimes the guilty). God bless you as you deal with this issue in your own Christian environment. Remember, only your submersion in the unconditional love of God and in his Word make you strong enough to break down the barriers of legalism.